Death in the Classroom

Death in the Classroom

A Resource Book for Teachers and Others

Eleanor D. Gatliffe

EPWORTH PRESS

British Library Cataloguing in Publication Data

Gatliffe, Eleanor D.
    Death in the classroom: a resource
    book for teachers and others.
    1. Death——Study and teaching——Great
    Britain
    I. Title
    306.9'07'041   HQ1073.5.G7

    ISBN 0–7162–0441–X

First published in 1988
by Epworth Press
Room 195, 1 Central Buildings,
Westminster, London SW1

Typeset at The Spartan Press Ltd,
Lymington, Hants
and printed in Great Britain by
Billing & Sons Ltd, Worcester

For Terry and Sue

Neither the sun nor death can be looked at with a steady eye.

La Rochefoucauld (1613–80)

Contents

Introduction

Some of the most difficult questions posed to adults by children are concerned with the child's attempts to understand death. This, like other aspects of the search for meaning, is a continuous process. An experience of death or loss may take place in early childhood and this and other experiences may give rise to an increasing number of questions as the child tries to make sense of what is seen and heard.

This book is about helping children, especially of adolescent age, to prepare for the reality of death. I feel that this can best be done within the framework of religious studies or religious education. I do not deny that such a task could also be approached within other subjects on the school curriculum – for example biology or home economics, but in this book I will attempt to show that death is a topic which can be dealt with effectively only in religious studies or religious education.

To deal with the concepts of death and life after death (sometimes referred to as 'beyonds to death') within such a context is, I think, important. For there is much more to death than that it is simply a biological fact. It is a reality which underlies much of our lives. Many great works of art, such as the Grand Portal depicting 'The Last Judgment' at the the Cathedral of St Etienne, Bourges, or Durer's paintings of the Apocalypse showing the pale rider on a pale horse (Rev. 6.8), 'King Death on a Horse', 'Death as a Ravisher', 'The Promenade', 'Death as a Fool', and so on, owe their creation to humanity's preoccupation with death. Literature too has been heavily influenced. Shakespeare presents a number of pictures of death, images of death, and death rhetoric. His treatment of death is dramatic and developed in the context of an entire play or plot; for example, both *Hamlet* and *Macbeth* are profoundly concerned with death.

> Nothing in his life
> Became him like the leaving it; he died
> As one that had been studied in his death

To throw away the dearest thing he ow'd,
As 'twere a careless trifle.

(Macbeth, Act I, Scene iv)

Emily Dickinson spent her life exploring death by means of poetry. She often personified death and regarded it as marriage, bride, king, tyrant, sleep, darkness, night and even comforter. Some of Dylan Thomas' poetry was profoundly influenced by his perception of death, for example, 'When Once the Twilight Locks No Longer', 'Do Not Go Gentle Into That Good Night', 'And Death Shall Have No Dominion':

And death shall have no dominion.
Dead men naked they shall be one
With the man in the wind and the West moon.

It has often been suggested that it is our fear of death which causes many of us to follow a particular body of religious beliefs. We hope that these beliefs will help to allay our fears, especially those concerned with what comes after death. Most of the major world religions believe that there is more to our existence than simply our period of life spent here on earth. Their beliefs are not, of course, identical for each faith has its own coherent belief system, and what any religion believes about death and beyond will be related to what it believes about God and the natural world.

It is important to mention here that a child's concept of death will be influenced by what it is taught. It is important, therefore, within religious studies or religious education to deal with all aspects and views of the subject, such as agnostic, humanistic, animistic, necromantic as well as those based on the major world faiths.

During my years of teaching I have become aware of the need to study this particular topic. Quite often in schools the subject is touched upon only very briefly within religious studies and perhaps not at all elsewhere. Although it might not appear to merit a course of lessons in its own right, it is a subject, I find, often raised in the classroom by children right across the secondary age-range, and at varying stages of academic ability. I have often found that children want and need to talk about their difficulties and fears in facing death.

This book is divided into two sections. The first part (chapters one to three) is designed to help prepare children in the school setting to cope with encounters with death. I have included selected examples from relevant research which has proved useful to me. Further discussion of this research is included in the appendices.

The second part (chapters four to six) sets out a structured approach to teaching about death. Possible goals for 'death education' which a teacher may want to pursue in the classroom, and the means to evaluate the achievement of these goals are also included. The term 'death education' refers to dealing with the issue of death and all its aspects within the school curriculum. In this book when I use the term I will be specifically talking about teaching the subject within the framework of a religious studies or religious education syllabus.

In chapter six I have suggested various ideas, methods and resources for use in the classroom which will augment teaching about death-related issues, and which I hope will enable the teacher to help children confront an especially difficult and important aspect of life.

Chapter 1
Background

Death and the awareness of death are two aspects of the human condition with which every culture must come to terms. Yet it is a subject which is evaded, ignored and denied by our youth-worshipping society. It is almost as though we have come to regard death as just another disease to be conquered. We *will* all die; it is just a matter of time. Death is as much a part of human existence as being born. It is one of the few things in life that we can be sure will happen.

During the sixties Geoffrey Gorer, an anthropologist, suggested that death had replaced sex as the unspeakable subject in the West. He said that death had become the new pornography, only spoken of if it could not be avoided and never in the presence of children. Sex, he believed, was becoming less taboo, and death, as a topic, was becoming more taboo.

In the past people mourned over the dead and took the process of mourning seriously. Grief was shown outwardly in special dress. Funerals were elaborate and on a fairly large scale; the coffin and corpse remained in the house from the time of death until the funeral. Friends and family came to pay their last respects. *Then* such observances were expected and accepted; today they would be regarded as morbid by the majority.

Before about 1900 a more logical attitude to death seemed to exist. In those days a significant number of babies could be expected to die before adulthood. Common childhood illnesses like whooping cough, diphtheria and scarlet fever were all obstacles through which one had to pass to reach maturity. Fatal accidents were common, and infections had to be allowed to run their course as antibiotics did not exist. Dying was visible; it was not romantic; it was often cruel and ugly, but it could not be ignored. Death was a frequent occurrence, a natural event which had to take place.

Today, as our standard of living has changed, so too has our attitude to death. A more impersonal view of death has become common. People do not mourn openly any more; grief is rarely shown publicly. It is considered bad taste. Funerals are kept simple and carried out with the minimum of fuss. Nowadays corpses are placed in 'Chapels of Rest' between death and burial or cremation. Very few families keep the body in the house during this time.

Yet even though our attitude to death has changed over the years, one thing has not changed. The human race has yearned for immortality since the beginning of time. Only the way in which we view this immortality has changed.

In the great religions of the East the doctrine of reincarnation expresses the cycle of birth, death and rebirth which is found in nature, but the doctrine affirms that through unending lives humanity may eventually find permanent union with the absolute, or the timeless peace of *nirvana*. The Old Testament parable of the Garden of Eden tells us that the tree of life stood in the garden; this suggests that people perhaps were destined for immortality but that they forfeited their chances by disobedience. Adam and Eve were cast out of Paradise 'lest he put forth his hand and take also of the tree of life, and eat, and live for ever' (Gen. 3.22, RSV). As people were sinful, it would be indeed terrible if they were to become immortal for they would possess powers which they could fearfully abuse. In this way the ancient biblical writers tried to explain both the fact of death and the contradictory longing for eternal life. There was no return from the dead. In Psalm 89.48 it is written, 'Who can deliver his soul from the power of Sheol?' (RSV). This was the place of the dead. It was a shadowy existence, terrible in its emptiness, and some even expressed the fear that Sheol was outside God's presence. 'The dead do not praise the Lord, nor do any that go down into silence' (Ps. 115.17, RSV).

There were however other strands of Hebrew belief about the afterlife. Many ancient peoples venerated their dead and relied upon them for counsel and advice. From early times until the advent of Communism, the Chinese were ancestor worshippers; the spirit of the dead parent or grandparent was considered an intrinsic element of everyday affairs. The Israelites were forbidden these practices because God was the only being worthy of worship. 'Let no one be found among you . . . who casts spells or traffics with ghosts or spirits, and no necromancer' (Deut. 18.10–11, NEB). Despite this we can see from the story of Samuel's visit to the witch of Endor that necromancy and witchcraft were a part of everyday life (I Samuel 28). This account provides evidence of a belief in the continued existence of the dead.

Burial customs were always important to the people of ancient times. Our knowledge gleaned from archaeology shows this. The human appears to be unique among animals in taking the trouble to bury the dead with ceremony, believing that this in some way affects the ultimate survival of the dead person. The Hebrews were no exception. It was important that the body did not remain unburied. The inhabitants of Jabesh Gilead, who were grateful to Saul, went by night to rescue his body and those of his sons, and anointed and buried them (I Samuel 31.8–13).

It is possible to trace a gradually growing belief in a more worthwhile survival in another world and in a resurrection to a new life on earth by tracing the changes in Old Testament thought through to New Testament times. Some scholars suggest that the passage found in Isaiah 26.19 shows a belief in the resurrection of the righteous to life on earth. 'But thy dead live, their bodies will rise again. They that sleep in the earth will awake and shout for joy; for thy dew is a dew of sparkling light, and the earth will bring those long dead to birth again' (NEB). In Daniel an explicit belief in the resurrection of the righteous is actually stated. 'Many of those who sleep in the dust of the earth will wake, some to everlasting life and some to the reproach of eternal abhorrence' (Dan. 12.2, NEB).

Gradually the belief in the resurrection of the righteous continued to develop, until we reach the New Testament period where we find the Pharisees holding a strong belief in the resurrection of the dead. They disagreed over this question with the Sadducees, who did not share their belief. On one occasion the Sadducees challenged Jesus about his own beliefs (Mark 12.23–33). According to the gospel writer, Jesus stated his conviction that there was a life after death, but pointed out that conditions in that life would be different from this one because the physical body was translated into a spiritual one. Mark also tells us that during the last months of his life Jesus predicted his own resurrection from the dead (Mark 8.31; 9.9,31; 10.34; 14.25).

The other gospels also give us evidence that Jesus believed in an afterlife. The thief crucified with Jesus was promised a place with him in paradise (Luke 23.43). Early Christians, following

Jesus in these beliefs, came to believe that because Jesus had risen from the dead the end of the world was near and with it would come the resurrection of those who had died before the end.

For all the New Testament writers resurrection was the gift of God which came to humanity through Jesus as Messiah. The last book of the Bible, Revelation, ends with the vision of a new Jerusalem, a heavenly city in which runs the river of the water of life. The tree of life stands by the river 'which yields twelve crops of fruit, one for each month of the year; the leaves of the tree serve for the healing of the nations' (Rev. 22.2, NEB). Death, therefore, was no longer the enemy, but the gate through which it was possible to pass to a richer, more complete life than anything experienced on earth.

Throughout the centuries people have sought an answer to the question of death and what comes after it. And we shall see that even now we continue to ask this question. In this society, where major technological advances in medicine have caused revisions in the criteria for death and the prolongation of the dying process, death is still feared by many people. Perhaps now more than ever there is a place for 'death education' in our schools. This must be concerned with the facts, skills, and attitudes we need in order to deal adequately with the meaning of death and with fears of death.

Chapter 2
Children and Their Response to Death

As adults we have learned to give reasonable and scientific answers to questions like, 'Why do we die?' 'Why do I die?' We have learned to separate the world into such compartments as reason, emotion, and belief. Yet the adult explanations fall apart when the façade of the rational self is removed by crisis or pain, and the child within us emerges. Many adults who are grieving or who learn that they are near to death may think of death as a punishment for some real or imagined wrong.

As children grow they pass through the process of developing conceptual models for understanding death; however, we must remember that there is no single mould into which all children fit. There seems to be no set of ideas which children inevitably have about death. Much diversity is present in children's ideas concerning death. Some researchers have concluded that the child's concept of death is developmental, following the same pattern as the evolutionary development of the species. They observe that children's answers to questions about death are similar to the answers given by pre-technological people when questioned by anthropologists.

Sylvia Anthony, a pioneer in the study of children's attitudes to death, disagrees with such views (see appendix one). She believes that children and pre-technological people draw logical conclusions from what they can observe in the world about them. For example, they perceive the body as being separate from the soul, for when we sleep at night we see and feel things that clearly do not require our bodily participation. Another observation is that everything a child can recognize as living also dies. Even those children who identify life with movement – clouds and the sun's daily path, for example – know that the clouds disappear and the sun goes away.

Another important factor influencing children in the formation of their ideas is the language that they use. Our slang is redolent of the imagery of death. If something is amusing we 'nearly die laughing'. If someone annoys us we tell them to 'drop dead'. If

5

we have had a tiring day we are 'dead tired'. Conversely, we try to avoid the use of words such as 'dead' or 'die' when we actually speak about death itself. Pets are 'put to sleep', people do not die, they 'pass on'. If adults shrink away from discussing death in straightforward terms with children it is little wonder, as we shall see, that children are fascinated by the concept of death and, in many cases, actually fear death – a fear which can remain throughout a person's life.

Studies in the field of developmental psychology by Jean Piaget and others have enabled us to recognize the relationship between children's thinking and how and what we teach. Piaget's research led him to identify the existence of five stages in the development of a child's thinking, each with its own distinct characteristics. These are mentioned briefly in the context of teaching about death.

For children at the pre-operational level (about eighteen months to five years) things are as they appear to be, and will remain so. Life is the experience of movement, and children attribute life to all things that move. So the concept of human life has no special importance. However, the absence of movement can denote the quality of death. When young children think about things which have died, they attribute to them all the qualities they had when they were alive. So the dead can be, for example, in the sky (heaven) drinking, eating, playing, carrying out a normal life as remembered by the child. The child can only grasp the known world; he or she probably assumes that his or her feelings about death are the same as adult emotions and so may try to comfort adults by sharing his or her ideas and feelings with them. For example,

A small child (4½) was told by her friend's mother that their pet rabbit (which had died that day) was in heaven with Jesus, and very happy. When her own grandfather died, noticing her own mother's grief, she attempted to comfort her by assuring her that grandad was very happy and with Jesus in heaven.

Children at the concrete-operational level (about five to ten years of age) are limited to specific causes and actual or possible occurrences but are able to separate the idea of death from that of their own death or the death of friends and family. Death at this stage is seen as final but far away and, as can be deduced from

Maria Nagy's research (see appendix one), it is usually personified.

At both the pre-operational and concrete-operational levels, death is often associated with sleep – a sleep which lasts forever. (See appendix one.) This idea is probably reinforced by adults when we use common euphemisms in our own language. The following examples are taken from *Death, Grief and Mourning in Contemporary Britain*, pp. 25–26.

> A 44 year old tool fitter from Scotland: 'I told my younger son that grandad was in a long sleep and was gone away to a happy land.'

> A 56 year old cleaning inspector (Church of England) from London: 'I just told them that Nanny had gone to sleep, you won't see her again.'

It has actually been reported that some childhood fears about death were focused on the prayer, 'Now I lay me down to sleep'.

The formal-operational level (about eleven onwards) is a stage at which some children are able to express thoughts on death which are comparable with adult ideas. Adolescents begin to express emotions more like the adult ones – denial, anger, depression – and many express a philosophical interest in the meaning of the concept of death. They may also question social customs or rituals at death, showing that they will not accept the adult view of the world without criticism. A fifteen year old pupil of mine questioned the amount of money spent on burials. 'It's just a waste of money. If somebody's dead, what do they know anyway? The money would be better spent on us. At least we would appreciate it!'

Ideas at this stage become more abstract. This was shown in a number of answers I received from children aged fourteen to sixteen, when I asked them the question, 'What does death mean to you?' (It must be noted here that the following examples were taken from children considered to be academically bright.)

> Jane (16): 'Death, to me, means the releasing of a soul from a worn-out body.'

> Michaela (15): 'Death, to me, is when the life passes out of something or someone and that person doesn't

7

exist as we know them any more, maybe they pass on to a better place, or maybe they're reincarnated or something.'

Linden (15): 'I think that death is the departure from one's earthly life. It is a time of sadness for the living; a time of happiness, I believe, for the dead person, as I feel they move on to a better existence.'

Samantha: 'The thought of dying doesn't scare me at all,
(14½) because I believe it's been planned for everyone. When you die I think you still "live on", doing the same things or maybe other things in another world.'

A great deal of research has been done on children's emotional responses to death. One piece of research was carried out by Maria Nagy. She attempted to form a connection between intellectual understanding and emotional response (see appendix one). She found that perhaps the most common emotion experienced by children when considering the concept of death is fear. My own research has shown this. (The examples below were taken from a selection of answers from about seventy mixed-ability children.)

Sam (13): 'When I think about death it really scares me. It upsets me to hear about people suffering or dying a slow death – it reminds me it could happen to me and I get frightened.'

Julie (12): 'Death must be a very lonely thing. I get very sad and scared when I think about my own death or of the death of someone who is close to me.'

Paul (12): 'Death scares me, because I do not know what there is after death. I know I've got to die, but I'd like to know about after.'

Studies involving older children have shown that fear and thoughts of death have helped us understand other aspects of adolescents' lives. It appears that the more intelligent and emotionally mature adolescent can deal with the concept of death better than those who have problems in other areas of their lives.

Adah Maurer came to this conclusion after asking 172 schoolgirls to write an essay about 'What comes into your mind when you think about death?' (See appendix one). She found that those less academically able had a greater fear of death, showing separation anxiety and remnants of beliefs in ghosts, as well as a preoccupation with disease and violence. These children usually made mention of physical things like the smell of corpses.

The research done on children's ideas about death and their emotional responses to death has shown us that often problems about the fear of death and thoughts about dying do not seem to exist by themselves but are connected with other problems in life. If a child is experiencing a difficult time at home or at school, there is more likelihood that child will also have some problems with death. However, this does not mean that every child has problems where the idea of death is concerned, but there is a chance that if one does have a problem with death, problems in other areas will also be present.

Fears of death seem to be closely connected with conflicts experienced by children. As we have already mentioned, often the problem will be related to anxieties concerned with separation, especially a fear of being separated from the mother. This problem is also related to a fear of abandonment. If a child has experienced the death of a parent, the fear of abandonment may become very real. This in turn may become self-blame, and the fear that the child itself caused the loss or abandonment. Fear of separation is less likely in environments where relationships are stable, although some psychologists say that each of us has such fears deep within our psyche. Where a child's relationships are not stable, fears of separation become central. For young children who lose a parent through death or divorce, the environment may prove to be unstable through this alone.

It would appear that many children seem to have a fear of death and do not fully understand the concept. On questioning adults about their ideas and beliefs it would also seem that they too, for all their adulthood, fear the thought of dying. This fear may be a reflection of a lack of encouragement during childhood to learn about death and dying.

Because of advances in medicine which have enabled people to live longer and healthier lives, death has more and more become something that is feared and misconceived. This attitude needs to be overcome. We need to encourage an understanding of the concept of death and dying and the grieving process, hoping to prevent the emotional upheaval and permanent damage which a significant death can cause a family as a whole.

Chapter 3
Helping the Child to Cope with Death and Dying

Children today are in a strange situation. They live in a time when the sight of natural death has been banished from everyday living, but also in a time when the nuclear bomb, the Nazi holocaust, images of famine and fatal accidents on television have made the prospect of death more imminent than at any time since the plague in the middle ages. They know that death is real, yet often they find it has an awkwardness attached to it; adults may not wish to discuss it. When death occurs, they don't know what to do.

As recently as the time of my grandparents, if a death occurred the community mourned. I recall my grandmother telling me of a time when, on the death of someone, people in the area (this could be classed as the street in which the deceased had lived and perhaps the surrounding streets through which the body would pass en route to the cemetery) would close their curtains. The streets were lined with straw, visits to the home of the deceased were made, grief was shared – all out of respect for the dead person. This sharing, my grandmother believed, made things easier to bear.

Today when a death occurs the rituals of death are often reserved for the family alone and often grief is kept private and not shared. Sometimes children are 'barred' from discussing death or the death of someone, therefore giving the impression that the subject is taboo. A friend of mine, who was eight years old when his grandfather died, recalls that whenever he entered a room where adults were talking about his grandfather or funeral arrangements, silence fell. When he asked questions, he was told vaguely that 'grandfather had gone away and wasn't coming back'. He was told not to talk to grandma about grandad as 'it would upset her'. From this experience he gained the impression that death was a topic which was not for open discussion and he was afraid to share and discuss with others any fears he had about death.

It is this attitude which I feel needs to be overcome. We must remember that even if children have not experienced the death of someone important to them, they may at least have experienced the death of a pet and that today it is not at all uncommon for scenes of death to be shown on television.

Another situation which sometimes arises is embarrassment caused by death. I have seen children who have experienced the loss of someone close to them feel somehow singled out by exaggerated attention to the death. This makes them feel embarrassed and as if they are on public display. Friends will not tell jokes or laugh in front of the child or may avoid meeting him or her because of discomfort over what to say. A past pupil of mine, after the death of a parent, told me she felt isolated from normal contacts and actually felt angry with her parent for dying because of the embarrassment it had caused her. She felt her friends were avoiding her and made herself ill to avoid attending school.

Children are not afraid to talk about death. From my own experience I have found they are willing to discuss the topic. In a religious studies lesson I have known the subject to arise from discussions about Christ's crucifixion and resurrection, or discussions about the Hindu belief in reincarnation, or from the study of Jewish mourning rituals. Sometimes the topic has inadvertently arisen or some pupils may have sought private conversation. They may sometimes begin with a flimsy excuse, but my feeling is that they are there to talk about something which is very important to them.

Occasionally, I find myself wondering if it is the right thing to teach about death. After all, it can be a very upsetting topic. I personally have had no resistance from parents when I have included the topic in my religious studies lessons. On the contrary, some parents have actually applauded the inclusion. However, some teachers who have decided to introduce the topic of death into the classroom may find that there is a resistance to what they are doing. This resistance may come from parents, or even fellow teachers, and may be based on the fear of death and the desire to stop thinking about it.

If resistance is met with, the teacher must address himself or herself to the parents. A good idea might be to do this before resistance even arises, perhaps by sending home a letter explaining what will be studied and giving reasons for the inclusion of death in the religious studies syllabus. For example:

Dear Parents,

Over the next few weeks we will be studying death and the process of dying. We will be learning the definitions of death used in medicine and law, and the kinds of decisions which patients, families and doctors sometimes have to make when people are dying. We will also be learning about social and religious customs and beliefs connected with death.

The death of someone close to your child can be a very difficult experience. Even if the death happened some time ago, your child might still be troubled. Please could you contact me if there is anything that it would be helpful for me to know about your child, or about circumstances in your family which may cause your child discomfort in studying the subject of death. I will, of course, keep whatever you share strictly private.

Death can be a terrible thing, but with the appropriate knowledge, it can sometimes be made easier to face. This is my purpose in introducing the topic to the school through religious studies lessons. If you wish for further details of the course of study, please do not hesitate to get in touch.

Yours sincerely,

If parents know exactly what areas are to be covered and the purpose for studying the subject they may feel better about their child discussing such a sensitive topic in the school setting. Some teachers may have difficulty sending such a letter on the grounds that the issue of death is singled out and becomes special in an undesirable sense, but I have found that this disadvantage is outweighed by the advantages I have already mentioned.

If the topic is included as a full course of lessons it must be dealt with, here as always, carefully. Grave problems could arise if the seriousness of the topic and the depth of feeling it may generate are not appreciated. As a teacher dealing with the subject in some depth I think it would be necessary for me to be prepared to follow through with pupils who appear to need extra time for private talks. If it became apparent that any pupil had strong anxieties about death I would feel obliged to alert others such as the school counsellor, who could then perhaps contact the family. Helping the pupil now may prevent future years of sadness. Anxieties about death can lead to later problems.

On discussing the problem with some groups of children I have found that many pupils have thought about their own deaths and some have faced the deaths of 'significant persons'. Like so many people they have been isolated with their thoughts and feelings by our culture's basic denial of death. Most of the pupils said that they simply tried to 'forget death will ever happen to anyone'. This is all very well, but death has a habit of entering our lives without waiting to be asked; we suddenly come face to face with it in a road accident or in the sickness and death of a friend or a member of our family.

When I discuss this aspect of death with my pupils I tell the story of the Buddha and his experience before Enlightenment. While out walking for pleasure he met with three experiences which he came to look upon as important revelations of the sad truth about life.The first 'sign' was an old man nearly bent double with age and sickness; the second was when he met a hermit who was seeking the answer to the problem of life. He then came across an old man who had died, his thin old body being carried to the funeral pyre. Here he realized that everyone, including himself, had to face suffering and death. Once the ashes were scattered there seemed nothing left of the person who had once lived. He was deeply shocked. He went home, his whole mind and body protesting the claims of life and health, but there was sickness, old age and there was death. And there was not only death, but mourners, a weeping wife, fatherless children – here were loss and separation too.

These experiences inspired the Buddha to go on to attempt to teach himself and others to understand death and to live in the presence of death in the noblest way. He taught his followers not to fear death but to go forward in their lives with great confidence, energy and calm, to care for those in sorrow and for those who feel bewildered at times of separation and loss.

The Buddha's teachings about death have been mentioned here very briefly. With my pupils I would deal with his doctrines in much more detail, to attempt to help them with their fears about death and loss. An important thing to remember if you are going to teach about death is that we ourselves are human. We face death ourselves, or losses which are significant to us (divorce, the loss of a job, a pet, and so on). If we handle the topic carefully and with sympathy we can offer our own experience to those troubled by death.

To deal fully with the topic we must be prepared to listen to what our pupils have to say. We must encourage them to talk and listen. Empathic listening may help them to talk more. Sometimes empathy will be difficult when we are very different from our pupils in age and background or personality. It is important, when the situation arises, that we do not simply project our own feelings. As we listen we must try to enter into the feelings they have. We have the advantage that because we have a wider range of experience we can put feelings and thoughts into the perspective of time. We must be careful not to jump at these situations when they arise with a fully loaded 'arsenal' of information which may be more than the child can understand or assimilate at once. We must give information at the level which the child can understand, and answer any questions asked as clearly and simply as possible.

Let me summarize the points made so far:

1. We can help children when they have problems with death.

2. We can listen and empathize.

3. We can respond with real feeling.

4. We can share our personal experiences and our life philosophy.

Most importantly we must remember that what we teach our pupils now may help them and, even more significantly, influence them for many years to come. I myself have had past pupils return to school two years after leaving, and tell me that they have found a lot of the subject matter we covered in religious studies helpful in their lives. So if we are going to teach such an important and sensitive topic we must plan an appropriate scheme of work with a great deal of care and thought.

Chapter 4

'Death Education' within Religious Studies or Religious Education

I have often spoken of 'death education'. I must make it clear at this point that when I use this term it is merely one of convenience which I employ to describe a unit of work concerning the study of death and beyond, designed for use within the framework of a religious studies or a religious education syllabus. From now on I will refer to the subject simply as religious studies. In this chapter I will attempt to explain why I believe the topic of death can be dealt with effectively within the framework of religious studies.

Belief in the survival of death is found in most religions and it is perhaps humanity's oldest religious conviction. Indeed, Arnold Toynbee believes that it is conceivable that some attitudes to death are innate in human nature. He tells us, in *Man's Concern with Death* (pp. 59–60) that 'the oldest, most numerous, and most imposing relics of our ancestors are funerary'. He goes on to say that however diverse human methods of disposing of the dead have been, they have all had something in common – 'they have signified that a human being has a dignity in virtue of his being human; that his dignity survives his death; and that therefore his dead body must not simply be treated as garbage and be thrown away like the carcase of a dead non-human creature'. In today's society this attitude of reverence towards the dead and with it the wish to give the dead a 'decent burial' continues.

There is a great variety of teaching about death and its consequences, from the belief in reincarnation held by the religions of India and beyond to that of bodily resurrection which predominates in Christianity and Islam. It has been suggested that our belief in our ability to overcome the limitation of death simply arose from wishful thinking. This could possibly be so, but attention must be given to the wider pattern of belief which surrounds such ideas, and all that it implies about the nature of God and people.

As I have previously mentioned, I believe it is important to give some attention to death within our educational system. It is unreal to ignore the topic totally, for it is so much a part of our lives and it is important for children to be given the opportunity to come to understand what beliefs people have with regard to death. By allowing children to study the deepest faith responses to the world in which they live and die, we may encourage them to come to terms with the major problems of living and dying. This knowledge, I believe, is as important as any which is scientifically based. As such it is important to do justice to the subject of death by studying both the religious and scientific viewpoints. It would not be fair to the pupils involved if only one aspect of any subject was presented. It will be seen that in chapter six I have looked at both the scientific and religious viewpoints concerning the subject of death. In an ideal situation perhaps the science department of a school could deal with one and the religious studies department with the other, working together to present the children with a clear, unbiased view of the subject. At the school where I teach, the subject of death is not dealt with anywhere in the syllabus in any detail. Therefore, I have planned a course of lessons to deal with both the scientific and religious points of view to match the needs, I believe, of my own pupils. Some of the beliefs which I feel it would be important to consider when teaching about death within a religious studies course are outlined below.

Hinduism

Indian and far-eastern religions are said to have a cyclic notion, teaching that all things move round in cycles of birth, death and rebirth, going on endlessly. Thus one of the symbols of Hinduism is the circle, representing the never-ending circle of life. This applies to the whole universe and it is believed in India that liberation or salvation can be obtained from this cycle or chain of rebirth, into the Hindu state of *moksha*, or salvation. This is the spiritual freedom which all Indian philosophers regard as the highest goal, the purpose of human life.

Belief in rebirth (reincarnation or the transmigration of souls) is characteristic of Indian religion. It seems probable that this was an ancient Indian belief, for it first appears in the Upanishads in about 800 BC A moral aspect of reincarnation appears in the doctrine of *karma*: those who have done good deeds in this life will be rewarded in the next. However, those who have been wicked will be reborn as pigs or as members of a lowly caste.

The doctrines of rebirth and of survival of death are based on the belief that one's soul (*atman*) is immortal and indestructible. The soul cannot die even when the body dies, and though it may be associated with many bodies in different rebirths during its journeyings, its true destiny is to get beyond this world into eternity.

Critics of this doctrine often say that we have no memory of previous lives, and therefore cannot profit from them, so that there is no proof that we are reborn. However, some people would put forward as evidence examples of people who, under the state of hypnosis, have seemed to regress to former lives. A good example of this phenomenon can be found in Jeffrey Iverson's book *More Lives Than One?* Here Iverson tells of a man called Arnall Bloxham who, over the years, had caused people to regress to former lives under the state of hypnosis. Over a period of twenty years he had recorded over four hundred examples of what he believed to be reincarnation. Under repeated sessions of hypnosis some of his subjects had regressed to as many as fourteen separate existences spread out over the centuries.

The author of the book listened to the tapes and actually watched some of Bloxham's subjects regress. He attempted to prove or disprove the regressions by carrying out historical research and found that the tapes seemed to have been corroborated. Arguments have been put forward against the genuineness of such material: the subject could have gathered the knowledge from a book or film; the hypnotist could have been responsible for transmitting the historical outlines of the regressions to the minds of the subjects; but these arguments have not been proved.

Many stories are told throughout the world of people meeting men and women with whom they had been closely associated in former lives; the Buddha is said, at his Enlightenment, to have looked back on all his previous lives. In Hinduism the belief in rebirth does not depend on memory, but on the conviction that the eternal soul was never born and can never be destroyed.

Judaism

Early Hebrew belief seemed to be concerned only with life on this earth, and it is true that a belief in resurrection did not appear until a late biblical stage. Despite this, there are some traces in the early parts of the Bible which show that the ancient Hebrews did have some notion of survival after death.

Graves, especially those of important people, often became shrines, sanctuaries and places of pilgrimage. For example, the bones of Joseph were carried to Shechem which was a holy place. Well-known phrases in the Bible speak of people 'sleeping with their fathers' and suggest, even if somewhat vaguely, that the dead joined their ancestors in death. Later there appeared the notion of Sheol, the place of the dead. Hezekiah said, 'I am consigned to the gates of Sheol' (Isaiah 38.10, RSV) and Psalm 88 reads, 'My life draws near to Sheol . . . like the slain that lie in the grave.' In Sheol it seems that man was not remembered for Psalm 88 continues 'whom thou dost remember no more' (RSV).

During the early history of Judaism the emphasis was upon living a good and righteous life here on earth, but it seems that the suffering and inequalities of life caused people to look beyond death for justification. Psalm 73 predicts trouble for the wicked and ends with confidence that God will 'afterward receive me to glory' (AV). In Isaiah 26 there is presented what seems to be a belief in resurrection, 'thy dead men shall live, together with my dead body shall they arise' (AV). In Daniel 12 there is a passage which seems to provide evidence of a developed resurrection belief: 'Many of those who sleep in the dust of the earth shall awake, some to everlasting life, and some to shame and everlasting contempt' (RSV). There is the notion here that the wicked will be punished while the good will be rewarded at the resurrection. However, some Jews did not believe in resurrection. The Sadducees for example denied its existence. However, the Talmud gives great importance to the resurrection of the dead and discusses many questions related to it. The thirteen Principles of Faith formulated by Maimonides (about 1172 AD) end with the words, 'I believe with perfect faith that there will be a resurrection of the dead at the time when it shall please the creator.'

Buddhism

Like Hindus, Buddhists also believe in reincarnation. However, Buddhist belief appears more difficult to understand than Hindu because of its negative teaching about the soul and the indefinable state of *nirvana*. Also, as in Hinduism, the condition of rebirth is thought by Buddhists to be determined by *karma*. Being linked with a new body depends on the deeds of the past life. Buddhists believe that the person who is reborn is not the same as the one who has just died, and yet the person is not different. They describe the state as being like the flame of a candle, which is not the same in the last watch of the night as it is in the first watch, yet the two are not separate. Two different candles are spoken of here.

The Buddhist notion of *nirvana* is believed to have begun with the Buddhists and the Jains; Hindus later adopted the word and it appears in the Bhagavad Gita. *Nirvana* literally means 'extinguished', 'calmed', and today it is sometimes explained as the extinction of the soul. However, this belief in the soul's being extinguished was never held by the early Buddhists or the Jains; they sought the extinction of all desires in the perfect calm of final bliss.

The nature of *nirvana* is hard to define, for Buddhists believe one cannot know its form or shape, its duration or size. A Buddhist would say that the Buddha still exists but that he cannot be located for he has attained the final *nirvana*. It is believed that *nirvana* ends suffering and gives joy and light; it is unspoiled and beyond all passions.

Such advanced spiritual teaching as this is difficult for the ordinary person to grasp. However, for the ordinary person there are still descriptions of heavens and hells in popular literature. Many of these are taken from the Hindu scriptures, where the heavens are described as beautiful places filled with beautiful things and beings. In contrast the hells are places where the damned are made to suffer; however, these sufferings are not eternal, for when one has paid fully for one's wickedness the soul may rise again, given another chance.

Christianity

Christian teaching is distinctive in its doctrine of the resurrection of Jesus Christ. The righteous who suffered were suddenly transformed by faith in his resurrection. Death was a fact, but early Christians spoke of death as a sleep. Christians were taught to rejoice in death for what they would gain through it.

In Corinthians 13 and 15 Paul seems to work out a theology of death. Parts of this are still used in funeral services. Death is connected with our first parents – 'as in Adam all die'. However, eternal life comes through Christ since 'in Christ shall all be made alive'.

Pictures of heaven and hell in Christian mythology were partly influenced by Jewish and Zoroastrian ideas. Hell was a place where the wicked would suffer eternal damnation, whereas the good would receive their reward in heaven. It is thought that during the early centuries of Christianity burial ceremonies were joyful affairs, celebrations that the person who had died had been released from mortal flesh and was now at peace, away from the trials and sufferings of life.

As time passed however attitudes to death underwent a change. It came to be believed that resurrection was no longer a certainty, but depended on God's judgment. Burial became an occasion for mourning. This change was emphasized by the Council of Trent (1545–1563) which decided that the sinfulness of human beings is so great that they will all need to be purified after death and this purification will be painful and take place in purgatory. Thus the Protestant and Catholic traditions of the Christian Church divided. Protestants were committed to the belief that God's atonement wrought in Christ was appropriated by belief in him in this life. Catholics were committed to the belief that cleansing was required after death even for the saved.

The majority of Christians today would reject the claim that life after death only comes to those who have declared their allegiance to Jesus Christ. It is quite inconceivable to most Christians that a loving God and the Father of all humanity should deliberately exclude the greater part of the human race from any hope of immortality simply because some nations happen to be outside the Christian Church's sphere of influence. Increasing knowledge of other great religions has helped Christians to believe that God must be at work within the religious life of humanity as a whole.

As I have already mentioned, the Apostles' Creed refers to

the resurrection of the body, and belief in this as a literal fact was once common. However, many Christians today would reject this idea, while maintaining that there must be a survival of some kind of 'spiritual body'. This would be needed to give a sense of continuity after death and a sense of personal identity. These Christians argue that if there were no bodily form we would neither recognize others after death nor continue to experience growth and development in the afterlife.

Other Christians would express their belief in a different way. They believe that eternal life begins here and now. If we can achieve a relationship with God through faith, we can experience the quality of eternal life in this world. At the raising of Lazarus, according to the gospel writer, Jesus said to Martha, 'I am the resurrection and the life, he who believes in me though he die, yet shall he live, and whoever lives and believes in me shall never die' (John 11.25–26, RSV). In this sense the person who finds God through faith in Jesus Christ is united to the source of love and life and therefore cannot be destroyed by physical death.

Islam

Orthodox Muslims would never doubt that there is a life after death. Early statements of belief declared faith in God, his angels, his books, his apostles, and the final resurrection. The doctrine of the last judgment is believed to be the second great tenet of the Qur'an, after the unity of God. This is the belief that after death people will be restored to life to appear before God, and assigned to paradise or hell according to their good or evil deeds.

Death is regarded as a simple certainty: 'Everyone is subject to death, and it is on the day of resurrection that you will be paid your rewards in full' (Sura 3.182). It is believed that the souls of the departed are taken into the charge of the angel of death and held until the resurrection. The interval will appear to them like only one day. Prayers will be said for the deceased, but only if they have died within the Muslim faith.

The last judgment will be the climax of history and it is described vividly in the Qur'an. It will be a day of upheaval, when God will appear and all human beings will be restored to life. This explains the Muslim aversion to cremation, for the body must be left intact if it is to be restored to life. The result of the judgment is paradise (*firdaus*), where the blessed will live, or hell (*jahannam*), which will be full of evil men and spirits who will undergo great suffering.

Sikhism

While Sikhism also teaches the unity of God, it has retained a belief in the deeply-rooted Indian notion of reincarnation. Guru Nanak spoke of people being born and dying, coming and going in the round of transmigration, and of the release which comes from union with the eternal Lord. A person's future life will be dependent on *karma*, but those who are fully devoted to God will be freed from this earth. This can be achieved by overcoming ignorance and wordly attachment (*maya*) and obeying the will of God.

Hell and heaven are states of mind and not geographical locations. They are symbolically represented by joy and sorrow, bliss and agony, light and fire. Sikhism has no conception of eternal damnation. Hell is the corrective experience taught through lower lives which the wicked will attain in rebirth. God has given complete freedom of moral choice to people to prefer hell to heaven and to prefer divine love to both hell and heaven.

Humanism

Humanists assume that death is the end of personal existence, for personality is seen to disintegrate with the onset of physical disintegration. The emphasis in humanism is placed on the doctrine that the ultimate values in the world are human. Most humanists are atheists, though they respect the Christian precept to love one's neighbour.

The humanist movement finds its roots in the religious scepticism of the eighteenth century. However, long before that there was Epicureanism, a philosophy which stressed moderation and indifference to the gods (who were thought to be indifferent to us). This school of thought was founded in Greece by Epicurus (342–270 BC).

The Epicureans made a special point of their teaching on death because of the superstitious fears of death which then prevailed. They did not celebrate funeral rites, and sought to eliminate the desire for immortality in any form (fame, for example) because they saw it as a source of anxiety. They believed the desire for immortality was destructive in that it spoiled the enjoyment of life.

This is not a negative attitude. It is rooted in taking the temporal conditions of all things seriously, as indeed the medium of all existence, the source and condition of all we hold precious. Not taking temporality as seriously as this is, in effect, contempt for life. In humanism creative activity is important; the emphasis is on working to contribute to the making of human life, with consequences that persist.

Death is hard to accept; the end of an unfulfilled life is especially tragic. Ceremonies may help the bereaved at this time to take final leave of the physical presence. However, like the Epicureans, modern humanists do not make much of funeral rites, or the disposal of the body. Instead they encourage friends and relatives to come together to contribute from their memories and impressions to the creation of a new image of the person they knew, cultivating what was produced during his or her life. In this way the dead live on, not immortal but as an influence still at work in the lives they shared.

Marxism

Karl Marx (1818–1883) charged that religion was the 'opiate of the people', and that it was an obstacle to progress. In a socialist society this world, and this world only, was a person's proper sphere. The values of religious experience were irrelevant. From Marx's writings came Marxism, which proposes itself as a rival to traditional religion. Although some would say it is rather like a religion, Marxism is explicity opposed to religions.

Marxism does have, however, a set of theories to explain the whole of reality and it has a policy for realizing a future 'heaven on earth'. Marxists believe that any struggling and suffering we undergo in this life will be compensated for in a better society for future generations. Our children will reap the benefits of any suffering we have experienced, and our memories will live on in our children.

As we can see, belief in the survival of death is widespread and enduring, and it is a belief which appears in many forms. Even in today's supposedly secular society many people still demand a religious service as part of the burial ceremony, and many still attend these services even if they do not understand or accept the doctrines behind the rituals performed. To avoid teaching about a phenomenon which we know to be universal is not sound educational policy.

In today's pluralist societies, where faiths are no longer isolated from each other, it is important that we all know about and respect the various beliefs of the major faiths. Children need to be prepared for living in the multi-faith society of which they are already members.

In religious studies children can be made aware of the religious understanding of life and their attention can be drawn to the central values such as courage, loyalty and honesty (many of them derived from religion) which society seeks to transmit. Children need to be taught about the transience and mystery of life which so many people perceive – some earlier than others. There is no greater mystery for humanity than death. Insight into life can be gained through reflection upon experiences such as birth, love and death. Only in religious studies can the child be provided with a basis for understanding the search for meaning in life which people have carried on since the beginnings of time. The subject of death can be looked at scientifically but a thorough grasp of the reality involved will only be developed if children are encouraged to analyse the concept in great depth, and allowed to place it within a wide context and so develop a clearer insight into this very difficult area.

Much work has been done on goals in education. In the Department of Education and Science pamphlet, *Curriculum 11–16* (pp. 42–44), it is stated that as a part of the school curriculum 'religious education shares with other subjects the task of helping children to acquire the skills, knowledge and social competence necessary for the personal development and life in society'. It demands that religious education should be concerned with what are called 'life's ultimate questions'. Among the questions can be included that of death and what lies beyond. The DES document also states that subject content must be related to the child's world and must help children to understand the world in which they live. If we are to do this within religious studies then we must look at what can be called the 'spiritual side of life'.

Examples of this 'spiritual side of life' can be found in the story of how Moses encountered God mysteriously in the burning bush, how Isaiah had a vision in the temple, and so on. These experiences may not all be historical, but there is little doubt that prophetic visions were central in the ongoing interplay between Yahweh and his chosen people. And in the early days of Christianity there is the experience of the apostles when they encountered the risen Christ; this experience transformed their lives. There is, too, the conversion of Paul which was essential to the spread of Christianity. A similar experience is found in Islam when Muhammed received Allah's message.

Such experiences do not always have to be as 'earth-shattering' as those mentioned above. They can occur on a smaller scale to individuals when what we preceive as 'the divine' erupts awe-inspiringly into our minds. Rudolph Otto, the German philosopher and historian of religion, believed these experiences were derived from what he called the *mysterium tremendum et fascinans*, 'the mystery which causes awe and which fascinates'. To such an experience he gave the label 'numinous' from the Latin *numen*, meaning 'a spirit'.

Another type of spiritual experience is that which comes from within. For example, we can see from the accounts of the Buddha's life that he received an inner enlightenment which he felt was essential to the attainment of liberation. It was indeed the ultimate source of the power of Buddhism, mediated through the teaching of the Buddha and his early followers who maintained the preaching of the *dhamma* (law). This 'interior vision' is vital to many forms of religious belief. It appears in Hinduism, early Taoism and Zen, in Islamic Sufism and in Christian mysticism.

There is always the possibility that our pupils may encounter such spiritual experiences and as religious studies teachers we must prepare them to understand and appreciate them. So by attempting to initiate pupils into this 'feeling side' of religion we hope that they may come to a closer understanding of such an experience as death. We hope, too, that we can bring them to a closer understanding of humanity's religious attitude to the subject and its place in our world. We should encourage all pupils to look beyond the facts and to search for a deeper meaning to death – only then will they truly come to understand why we have placed such an importance on the event and perhaps come closer to understanding their own beliefs and ideas about death.

Chapter 5
Goals in 'Death Education'

What kinds of goals do I have for the children whom I teach? I believe that my goals must go beyond the straightforward imparting of facts – what Christians believe about life after death, how Muslims bury their dead, or how the Jews prepare their dead for burial. We must attempt to help our pupils to *understand* these facts and to examine their responses to the idea of death.

There are different dimensions of 'death education'. One takes place within the family context, and the other within the structured context of the school setting. Yet I believe the goals are basically the same for each. One dimension exists when the school socializes within the general culture, another when the family transmits its particular values, attitudes and traditions. However, the relationships formed at school with teachers and friends in the playground have a different emotional quality from relationships at home. Also, there is a difference between the learning process of the school, in both the regular and the hidden curriculum, and the informal learning process that occurs within the family.

The goals we choose for our pupils will be our answer to what we want them to get out of 'death education'. I will be teaching the subject within the framework of religious studies, so of course this will affect the goals I choose. However, no matter how formally we state our goals, the teaching of the concept of death presents some special challenges, because of the very nature of the subject. By establishing goals, the process of planning activities and gathering resources becomes easier, for we have a standard by which we judge ideas and materials. If we know our goals, it will be easier to evaluate our teaching, because all we have to do is find out if we have accomplished what we set out to do. After careful thought I have devised four general goals around which I would structure 'death education' within religious studies:

1. To inform pupils of, and to help them to understand, the facts of death and dying.

2. To help pupils to formulate the socio-ethical issues related to death, and to define the value judgments these issues raise.

3. To inform pupils of, and to help them to understand, the many beliefs and practices concerning death and beyonds to death.

4. To enable pupils to understand the various medical services available and to make them informed consumers of funeral services.

The last point may seem a strange choice for a course of work set within the framework of religious studies. However, 'death education' (apart from the mention in history lessons of the number of deaths caused by plague, disease and insanitary conditions and how the situation has improved over the years) does not exist in the school where I teach. So there is a real need to inform pupils of the many aspects of the topic and to give an idea of the issues such as euthanasia, organ donation, suicide and so on which are under discussion in society today. I believe it is important to give the pupils as wide a background knowledge of a subject as possible, if they are to gain a full understanding of that subject.

These general goals are interrelated, for the material that is covered in approaching one goal may necessarily be part of another. For example, a knowledge of the basic facts about death would be essential to all the goals. Furthermore, if pupils are given a chance to examine their responses to the idea of their own death and the death of others who are significant to them, they will be more able to examine socio-ethical issues. I have outlined each goal, given a brief sketch of the material used in approaching that goal and some guidelines for evaluation.

1. To inform pupils of, and to help them to understand, the facts of death and dying

The aim here is to provide some answers to the question, 'What happens when people die?' Sometimes death is a taboo topic for discussion. This means that there is quite often widespread ignorance of such facts as the legal and medical definitions of death, the effects of advancing medical technology on the span of life, common hospital practices concerning the dying and their families, the nature and cost of funeral services, appropriate social and religious rituals at the time of death, and the ways of coping with death which obtained in other times and cultures.

Questions that pupils ask are worth exploring, because they ultimately point to the pupils' curiosity and fears about their own deaths and those of their families and friends. Some people may find it difficult to speak to their own children about death because of their own fears and ignorance concerning the subject. This could actually cause parents to resist their children being taught about death. If this attitude did arise then the teacher would have to meet the parents to discuss the problem, and try to convince them that the subject is studied for the good of their children. If they refused to be convinced then the child in question would have to be removed from the religious studies lessons, as is the parent's right. To avoid such a situation arising a letter could be sent to the parents explaining why the teacher feels it is important to include the subject of death in the syllabus. The procedure is described in chapter three.

Evaluation: If this goal has been achieved the pupils should be able to demonstrate a knowledge and understanding of essential factual material at their own cognitive level. They should also be able to show a knowledge and understanding of the basic biological and psychological processes surrounding death.

2. To help pupils to formulate the socio-ethical issues related to death and to define the value judgments these issues raise

Here there are important questions of social policy and ethical practice which must be examined. Before discussion the teacher must admit to the class that none of these questions can be answered easily. Listed below are some questions for the teacher to think about.

1. Given limited medical and economic resources, should great efforts be made to maintain the lives of the old and sick who may be functioning at extremely low levels?

2. What is our definition of life? Do we consider length of life (quantity) more important than high-level functioning (quality) for a limited time?

3. Is the current trend towards private mourning rituals consistent with creating and maintaining caring communities?

4. What is euthanasia? Who has the authority to decide whether a person lives or dies? Discuss arguments in favour of and against voluntary and compulsory euthanasia.

5. Should funerals be 'big business'?

All these questions are important and they are all concerned with issues which are becoming more and more common in our society. For example, at a time when the funds available to the National Health Service are limited, it has been argued that to keep people with brain-damage alive is an unnecessary drain on resources. The media have recently documented a number of cases in which euthanasia has been given to aged and/or sick people by their friends or close relatives. Such cases are now occasionally looked upon more sympathetically by the courts who, in the past, have imposed heavy punishments or even charges of manslaughter.

The issue of suicide could also be included in this part of the course. Until 1961 it was a criminal offence to commit suicide or to attempt to do so. In that year the Suicide Act was passed without opposition, which removed suicide from the sphere of the law. But it remains a criminal act, punishable by fourteen years imprisonment, to aid or advise suicide. Conversely, whereas many westerners tend to look on suicide as a sin, there are occasions in eastern cultures where it is seen as a highly noble act on the part of the protesting monk, the defeated Japanese warrior, or the loving wife. In the past the good Hindu widow burnt herself to death in order to go with her husband to the next existence. The British stamped on the custom, known as *suttee*.

The questions outlined above can be rephrased to match the academic level and emotional maturity of the pupils. If social and ethical issues are to be discussed, the teacher must have a firm grasp of the complexity of the issues involved. If discussion were to take place and the teacher was not sure of the facts this could harm the pupils rather than help them. Older pupils especially will be able to make judgments about these questions. I personally deal with such issues with children of the upper-secondary age-range from about fourteen to sixteen years of age. I believe the teacher must help his or her pupils by supplying them with sufficient information for making judgments. As these issues are now commonly being raised in our society, especially the question of euthanasia, it would be advantageous for teachers to watch the media for material which can be used as a basis for discussion.

Evaluation: Students should be able to demonstrate a knowledge and understanding of the socio-ethical issues related to death and dying.

3. To inform pupils of, and to help them to understand, the many beliefs and practices concerning death and beyonds to death

An important area of study is the way in which people respond to and cope with a traumatic loss. Children need to know how people behave when they grieve and in what ways our society provides the means to express natural and healing displays of grief. This will help them understand those around them as well as the meaning of pain and loss when they look seriously at their own grief.

It is also important to consider the effect of death on the social and religious groups surrounding an individual and the ways in which various societies respond to death. To this end social and religious rituals associated with funerals and the mourning period can be investigated historically and cross-culturally. These could be examined by exploring the different practices of the various ethnic groups represented in the classroom. As part of the study of death customs in their own culture pupils can play the various roles of family, friends, pall-bearers, clergy and so on. For example, the death ceremony in Sikhism could be role-played. At the death-bed of a Sikh, the relatives and friends console themselves and the departing soul by reading *Sukhmani,* the Psalm of Peace. When death occurs, no loud lamentations are allowed. Instead, the Sikhs exclaim, *'Wahiguri, Wahiguri!'* (Wonderful Lord!). The dead body is washed and clothed (complete with the five symbols) before it is taken out on a bier to the cremation ground. Prayers are said and suitable hymns are sung on the way. Placed on a pyre, the body is set alight by the nearest relations. When the fire is burning fully, someone reads *Sohila* and offers prayers for the benefit of the dead. As people leave, they are thanked by the dead person's relations and dismissed. The bereaved family will read, for the comfort of their own souls and the benefit of the departed, passages from the Holy Book.

The role play of such ceremonies does not, of course, require the presence of a member of the faith in question to be carried out. The pupils involved and the remainder of the class could follow the role play with a discussion of the etiquette, responsibilities and possible feelings of the people whose roles were played. If this were done it would give the pupils an idea of the different religious customs which are practised. I personally found this approach very successful and it provided valuable material for discussion.

It is essential that different social and religious ideas of beyonds to death are discussed at this point. When discussing the concept of death with my own pupils a question which is constantly raised is, 'What happens after death?' Many of the children felt they would not be so afraid of death if they could be sure that there was something afterwards.

The children's own beliefs and fantasies about what happens after death can now be explored. General religious ideas such as resurrection, heaven, reincarnation, afterlife and so on must all be raised, for all religions have something to say about death and beyond. A discussion of such ideas will show that fears and ideas about death are a shared human experience. It is important that the teacher does not attempt to assure the pupils that life after death does actually exist; it is the teacher's role to initiate and guide the discussion and, if necessary, offer alternative ideas to those being passed round.

We must remember at this point that we can probably never take away the fear of the pupil's own death, for that fear is realistic – we will all die some day. Nor can we take away completely the pain which the pupils may have experienced as a result of the deaths of others. We can only attempt to share feelings, thoughts and beliefs. We cannot assure the children with certainty that there is life after death, but we can open up the different views held by others, including those of the many faith communities, which they may be able to use as a 'healing force' in their own lives.

Resistance to 'death education' may arise when discussing different religious customs and ideas concerning death and beyond. Parents may argue that what is being taught is against their own religious ideas and beliefs. If such a problem did arise then the teacher would have to convince the parents that all the religious questions would be dealt with equally and with sensitivity. At no time must a teacher attempt to convince the pupils that one particular system of religious belief is the most important or acceptable. As teachers, we must introduce topics for discussion, attempt to guide these discussions along the most rewarding course, and, whenever possible, share our own ideas, beliefs and experiences with our pupils.

Evaluation: It is very difficult to evaluate effective learning. We will not be sure how much of the material imparted will have helped the pupils until death and grieving affect the child directly. However, some idea will be given when discussing the topic and discovering, from what the pupils say or from their written work, whether or not their awareness and understanding of the concept has increased.

4. To enable pupils to understand the various medical services available and to make them informed consumers of funeral services

Today many people die in institutions, surrounded by life-sustaining medical equipment. Our individuality is often lost within the institutional framework. In order to combat this problem, pupils should learn to be responsible for family and personal care by exercising their legal rights within health care systems. Modern medical technology allows the doctor to make decisions about painful treatments which the patient and family may not wish to have. Doctors today do seem to be more willing to enable the patient and family to share these decisions. However, some people stand in awe of doctors, assuming that the doctor knows best, and are afraid to disagree with the doctor's decisions.

Knowledge of the legal restraints under which the medical profession works will prove useful to people who find themselves in the position of disagreeing with a doctor about a particular type of treatment which is being considered. Moreover the medical definitions of death must be considered when one is teaching this topic. Pupils should be presented with the facts about organ donation, the moral and ethical issues attached to the whole practice and then be encouraged to explore their own ideas about the subject. It is an issue which is currently under discussion in our society.

Just as they are unfamiliar with medical services, many people are also unfamiliar with the procedures for organizing a funeral. Yet, at some time in their lives, most people will find themselves in the position of having to do this. So it will be useful for pupils to learn something about the services that the funeral director can provide to both family and community. Pupils should be encouraged to explore their own values and to communicate with family members about funeral traditions and about what family members desire for themselves.

Reference could be made here to the universality of burial procedures and the diversity of the ceremonies, customs and beliefs attached to these. We know from archaeology how important the burial of their dead was to ancient peoples. The human race appears to be unique in taking the trouble to 'dispose of' the dead with ceremony, believing that this in some way affects the ultimate survival of the dead person. The diversity of these procedures is clear when one considers that in the late nineteenth century the introduction of cremation to England was greeted with ferocity by many! Such a situation would not, for example, have arisen in India where the Hindus had been cremating their dead for thousands of years (and continue to do so). In England, at that time, only the bodies of the 'godless' or heretics were burned at death. As John Bowker says in *The Sense of God* (p. 69), 'The variety of burial customs . . . reflects the various ways in which men have sought to scan and penetrate the limitation of death. . . . Burying a body gains suggestive confirmation from the burying of a seed and the growth of a new plant. . . ; burning a body gains suggestive confirmation from the observation that the burning of anything releases something (visibly in smoke) into the air and leaves only a changed and much smaller part of whatever was there in the ashes; floating a body out to sea, or committing it to a river, gains confirmation from the observation that salt dissolves in water, but, from the taste of the water, it is apparent that it has not wholly disappeared.'

I have given some examples of ways in which certain groups and societies have attempted (or still attempt) to overcome the limitations of death, showing that they refuse to accept it as the end. Usually these examples of our setting ourselves against the limitation of death are accompanied by various rituals and customs – many of them religious. For the pupil to gain a full understanding of funerary customs and rites the whole spectrum must be considered – including the practices of people who decline a religious service preferring a 'civil' ceremony, which usually involves friends and family carrying out readings, occasionally chosen by the deceased. The teacher must encourage the pupil to explore all these possibilities.

Evaluation: If this goal has been reached, pupils should be able to show where to find appropriate information on funeral and medical services and demonstrate some knowledge of the choices available. They should also be able to discuss the kinds of decisions they may face in the future.

Reaching or approaching these goals may help the pupils to overcome some of the problems faced by many of us when we consider the concept of death. These problems may include an ignorance of the basic facts of our world, an inability to deal with death when confronted with it, the lack of information for making basic consumer decisions and the lack of value-concepts to deal with the social and ethical issues death presents. Overall, our pupils should be encouraged to accept that death is, in fact, a part of life and, as such, should not be feared.

Chapter 6
Suggested Curriculum Content for the Teacher's Use in 'Death Education'

This chapter is a guide for the use of teachers as they plan lessons in 'death education' within the framework of religious studies or religious education. It is by no means exhaustive; I do not suggest I have listed everything that can be done. All teachers know their own pupils and their own teaching strengths, so the suggestions I make could possibly be adapted to other teachers' styles and their pupils' needs.

I have arranged these suggestions so that each has an objective, a list of activities and then a list of resources for the use of the teacher and the pupil. I do not claim to have found every book or audio-visual aid there is, but I have listed those I know of, or have actually used.

As I mentioned earlier, the particular age-group to which I would find myself teaching the subject of death, within religious studies, is from fourteen to sixteen years of age. So this unit of work on death is aimed towards that age-group in particular. However, I do think that some of the suggestions could be used, if adapted, with younger children. Obviously, all teachers will find there is a limited amount of time they can give to any one subject. With such a subject as death I believe about a term (usually thirteen weeks) would be an adequate amount of time.

In my present situation I would use two thirty-five-minute sessions per week. I have devised the unit of work to deal with many issues, such as old age, euthanasia, organ-donation, and suicide, as well as some of the existing religious beliefs and customs. The amount of time devoted to each of the issues raised would depend on the teacher in question, on the degree of importance placed upon the particular issue by the teacher, on the response of the group of children being taught and the interest shown by the group. All these points, and especially the last one, would be instrumental in deciding the length of time given to each issue in question.

I would hope that as well as becoming familiar with the facts, the pupils would gain some insight into the concept of death, therefore furthering their own understanding, although this insight might only come in later or post-school years.

It is once again important to emphasize the need for the teacher to appreciate the seriousness of the subject involved. Risks are involved in the teaching of death, because children are aware of the ever-present threat of death. Some pupils may be upset by discussion of the subject and the teacher must anticipate this by preparing a carefully-planned course of work on death and dealing with the subject with extreme sensitivity.

Suggested Curricula for the Teaching of the Topic of Death within Religious Studies

Objective: *To explore the pupils' own feelings about the aged and about getting old*

Activities

1. Encourage pupils to discuss among themselves the oldest person they know. Identify what they perceive old people as able to do and not able to do. The teacher could distinguish here the limitations of age (i.e. senility, and its effect on memory recall and the person's sense of identity, changes in bodily function effected by old age) from the limitations of disease.

2. Discuss how ageing persons in the pupils' families are cared for and how their special needs (i.e. living conditions) are catered for. Spotlight examples of the aged who still live, work and function in the community/society. Famous examples could be used here, for example, Ronald Reagan, the Queen Mother, Lawrence Olivier, Mother Teresa.

3. Play to the pupils recordings of old people's personal reflections on being old and being close to death. I would use here a sheet, which I have compiled, of some old people talking about their own lives and their thoughts on being old (see appendix three, 'Voices') and discuss any questions raised by the pupils. I would also use the poem: 'A Crabbit Old Woman Wrote This' (see appendix three) and ask the pupils what they think the 'Old Woman' of the poem is trying to communicate. The song 'Old

Friends', by Paul Simon, may also prove a useful source of discussion.

4. To help the pupils to understand some of the physical limitations of the aged, select some of them to try any or all of the following activities:

(a) Place cotton wool in their ears.
(b) Tie lollipop sticks to their fingers.
(c) Tape tennis balls on the inside of each knee cap.
(d) Wear a pair of thick-lensed glasses.

Encourage the 'impaired' pupils to interact with the 'normal' pupils and attempt normal activity. Discuss what happens.

5. If possible it would be useful to take the pupils on a visit to an old people's home. Ideally, regular visits would be made throughout the term, allowing the pupils interaction with old people. It would be best if some constructive activity could be planned. Some pupils could perhaps help in looking after the old people or simply in keeping the old people company. If such visits could be arranged on a regular basis the pupils involved could keep a diary for discussion about what is learned from such a place and the people there. The carrying out of such an activity would depend on the size of the group of pupils involved.

Resources

Sheet 1: 'Voices', consisting of old people giving their views on life and their feelings on being close to death (appendix three).

Sheet 2: 'A Crabbit Old Woman Wrote This' (appendix three).

Song: 'Old Friends', Paul Simon, *Bookends*, 1971.

Tapes: recording old people's personal reflections – preferably with accompanying sheets.

Objective: To find out what causes death

Activities

1. Pupils cut out articles from magazines or newspapers on the various causes of death, i.e. famine, disease, road accidents, air disasters, natural disasters, murder.

2. Pupils display and discuss the material which they have collected. Collage work could be done and entitled 'Causes of Death'.

3. Discuss life expectancy and how it has changed over the years. (Here the facts of death caused by famine in the Third World could be included, although I would personally deal with this in a separate unit on world poverty.)

4. Discuss whether or not the media (television, newspapers, films, cartoons) portray death in a realistic fashion. Conduct a survey and discover what pupils most commonly watch on television. Ask the pupils to watch the most popular programmes in one specific period; the teacher must also watch. If possible video record these programmes and allow the pupils to watch together. The following questions could then be discussed:

(a) To whom does death occur?

(b) How does death occur?

(c) Is death related to concepts of good and evil? Are good deeds rewarded with life and bad deeds punished by death?

(d) Is death presented realistically?

(e) Is the reality of death denied?

(f) Does television mirror the pupils' life experience?

(g) Are any concepts of an afterlife common in our culture?

(h) How are these concepts related to social values?

5. Discuss the pupils' past experiences in connection with death and how they remember feeling at the time.

6. Ask the pupils to recall their earliest death-related experience (include the death of pets) and record in a written assignment how they were affected.

Resources

Newspapers, magazines.

If possible, examples of death portrayed or taking place in cartoons, films and the news or documentaries.

Objective: To introduce pupils to the facts about institutions which are concerned with death

Activities

1. The teacher must present various places where death may take place and provide information about each, i.e. the hospital, the nursing-home, the hospice, the home.

2. The pupils must learn about the role of the modern hospital in the process of dying. If it is possible, invite a member of the medical profession to talk to the pupils about life-prolonging measures in a hospital, daily hospital routines etc.

Objective: To help the pupils explore their own feelings about death and dying and their own ideas of beyonds to death

Activities

1. Ask the pupils to write down their own ideas concerning death and beyond without any preliminary discussion.

2. Introduce material such as I have included in sheet 3, 'Children's Experiences of Death' (appendix three).

3. Discuss the ideas which the children have written down. If there are any volunteers, let them read out their work. Are any of the ideas of the class similar to those expressed on sheet 3?

Resources

Sheet 3: Children's Experiences of Death (appendix three).

Book: *Death*, Mog Ball.

Objective: To explore further the pupils' own feelings about dying and beyonds to death by carrying out a cross-cultural study of beliefs and customs about death

This is in order to acquaint pupils with a broad range of views and practices concerning death, both religious and non-religious.

Activities

1. Have the pupils draw their own idea of what death is. Show them some common cultural symbols of death (e.g. the Reaper, a

skull and crossbones, an avenging angel, a skeleton). Discuss the meaning of the drawings with the pupils and then allow them to illustrate their own symbol of death, also explaining its meaning.

2. Take the pupils to visit a cemetery. Invite them to look at and record the varying shapes of gravestones and some epitaphs. Discuss what these things tell us about other people's beliefs and customs.

3. Study some ideas about death and beyond from selected faiths. Here I would follow the policy of including the world's major faiths: Hinduism, Judaism, Buddhism, Christianity, Islam and Sikhism. I would also, for variety and for the sake of comparison, include humanism and Marxism.

(a) In a study of attitudes to death and what lies beyond it, not only beliefs concerning the subject are involved, but also funeral liturgies and burial customs, for these will also reflect attitudes to death.

(b) Before studying the beliefs of separate faiths some common beliefs and ideas must be explained. For example, the idea of resurrection is present in Christianity, Judaism and Islam, whilst belief in reincarnation is present in Hinduism, Buddhism and Sikhism. It is important to explain specifically what these two terms mean. Some information about these concepts must be given and this can be followed by allowing pupils to discuss and then write about their own beliefs and ideas. If possible allow pupils to listen to excerpts from the 'Bloxham Tapes', and passages from *More Lives Than One?* could be read to them by the teacher. Ask them to consider whether or not they would agree that this could be used as evidence for reincarnation.

Resources

Tapes: The 'Bloxham Tapes'.
Book: *More Lives Than One?*, J. Iverson.

A scheme of work for Hinduism

1. Discuss the Hindu idea of the soul. Show extracts from Hindu literature which describe this concept. Describe the Hindu attitude to life; once again extracts from the literature can be used.

2. Discuss the concept of *karma* – the moral law of cause and effect. Ask pupils if they believe that how they act in this life will affect what happens to them beyond death. (This is if they believe in life after death.) Do their beliefs actually affect the way they act and live now? Consider yoga.

3. Discuss the funeral ceremony and in what ways it differs from the practices of other cultures. Show pupils some prayers recited at the ceremony (appendix three). What do these teach us about the Hindu's attitudes to death?

Resources

Sheet 4: The Hindu Attitude to the Soul (appendix three).
Sheet 5: The Hindu Attitude to Life (appendix three).
Sheet 6: Prayers Recited at the Hindu Funeral Ceremony (appendix three).

Books: *A Hindu Family in Britain*, P. Bridger.
　　　Life Among Hindus, D. G. Butler.
　　　The Way of the Hindu, Swami Yogeshananda.

A scheme of work for Judaism

1. Describe how, in Judaism, death is seen as one stage on a 'Path of Life', as part of the destiny of the individual. Discuss what we can learn from this point of view.

2. Death in Judaism is accepted as the community's responsibility and the 'Holy Fraternity' is organized to supervise and carry out all rites and arrangements connected with death and burial. Discuss its duties and what use the pupils believe similar organizations could serve in our own society.

3. Describe how the body is treated after death; note the great respect it is given. The mourning period of the close relatives of the deceased reflects this respect. Refer to the sheet entitled 'Mourning in Judaism' (appendix three). Discuss whether or not the pupils believe such demonstrations are necessary – how could they help the deceased? A comparison can be made here of how members of our culture grieve for their dead; grief is usually a private thing, often too embarrassing to be discussed. Consider whether we can learn anything from the Jewish mourning practices.

43

4. Belief in the afterlife and resurrection are prevalent in Jewish faith. Discuss the forms these beliefs take.

Resources

Sheet 7: Mourning in Judaism.

Books: *A Jewish Family in Britain*, Vida Barnett.
Landmarks in Life, C. Brittain and M. G. Treddinick.
Problems of Christian Living, E. J. Taylor.
The Way of the Jews, Rabbi Dr Louis Jacobs.

A scheme of work for Buddhism

1. Here some knowledge of the Buddha's early life is necessary if one is to understand fully the Buddhist idea of death. Special note should be made of the Buddha's Enlightenment. This story can be used to help the pupils to cope with the idea of their own death, by accepting that we must all die.

2. The Buddhist perception of death can be difficult and must be described carefully if the pupil is to understand it. We must explain here that the Buddhist attitude is very different from our own and comes from a different world-view. To understand it we must attempt to enter this world.

3. Discuss the Buddhist ideas of rebirth and *nirvana*, and how we ourselves determine our fate in the next life. Pay special attention to the state of *nirvana* – how does this compare with the pupils' own ideas of the afterlife?

4. Refer to the sheet entitled 'The Buddhist Funeral Service'. Discuss whether or not the pupils find such a service attractive or whether it is too alien to western culture.

Resources

Sheet 8: The Buddhist Funeral Service.

Books: *Buddhism*, T. Ling.
The Way of the Buddha, C. A. Burland.

A scheme of work for Christianity

1. The Christian Church has always said that physical death does not necessarily mean the end of existence. When a Christian dies

the family mourns the loss of a loved one. However, Christians should not be anxious about meeting death, for it is a state in which they will finally be with God. The theme, therefore, of a Christian funeral service will be hope. In this Christians are following the teachings of Jesus, who himself returned from the dead, and appeared to his friends to show that God gives life after death. Paul's writing on resurrection (I Corinthians 15) can be introduced here.

2. Before death Catholics receive the sacrament of Extreme Unction – the anointing with oil by a priest to bless them. This is very important, for an emphasis is placed on the unity of body and spirit which points towards a resurrection in these terms. The last communion is also received; this is to prepare the person who is dying for the journey ahead.

3. It is difficult to say what the afterlife is like, but its essence is being in the presence of God. Jesus did not say much about it. Catholics believe in a state called purgatory. Here the soul is cleansed by some form of suffering; this suffering will depend on the measure of a person's imperfection.

4. Consider the feast of All Saints which is celebrated by both Protestant and Catholic traditions. This takes place on 1 November, and is when all Christian saints are remembered. The feast of All Souls should also be mentioned; this is celebrated on 2 November, and is the remembrance of all departed Christian believers.

5. For comparison's sake mention could be made of the beliefs and ideas concerning death of one of the Free Churches. Below I will describe those of the Methodist church.

Christian Funeral Customs

1. The practices of both the Protestant and Catholic churches are similar, but the words used differ. The funeral usually takes place within four to five days of death. The body is washed and dressed in normal clothes. The coffin approaches the church followed by mourners, traditionally dressed in black. The priest greets the coffin with the words, '"I am the resurrection and the life," says the Lord.'

2. The priest will give a brief talk about the person who has died.

The prayers speak not only of sadness but also of joy and hope because of the Christian belief in life after death.

3. The body is then either buried or cremated with more prayers being said. If cremation takes place, either the ashes are scattered, sometimes in a place of the deceased's choice, or they are buried.

4. In the Methodist tradition the funeral service will usually take place in a church. The service tends to be similar to those of other Christian traditions. Sheet 10, 'The Methodist Tradition' can be referred to here.

5. Refer to the sheet entitled, 'The Christian Funeral Service'. Note that the passage in Revelation 21 is used. This passage assures us that there are no conditions of entry into God's kingdom. Everything is left in the hands of God. 'I am Alpha and Omega, the beginning and the end. I will give unto him that is athirst of the fountain of the water of life freely' (Rev. 21.6, AV).

NB. Teachers can at this point draw attention to the similarities between the three different services as well as remarking upon the differences.

Resources

Sheet 9: The Christian Funeral Service.
Sheet 10: The Methodist Tradition.

Books: *Perspectives*, M. A. Chignell.
Problems *of Christian Living*, E. J. Taylor.

A scheme of work for Islam

1. Stress the simplicity of the Muslim attitude to death – human beings live, die and rise again (see appendix three, 'Muslim Death Rites').

2. Show passages from the *Qur'an* reflecting the Muslim idea of death, and the prayers and readings used during a funeral.

3. Discuss the funeral practices of Muslims i.e.

(a) The preparation of the body.

(b) The gathering of relatives and friends at the home of the deceased to help comfort the immediate family.

(c) The carrying of the coffin to the mosque or burial ground and the saying of the prayer – *salat-ul-Janazah*.

(d) The coffin faces *qiblah* – towards Mecca.

(e) The congregational funeral prayer involves no bowing or prostration. The *Al-Fatiha* – the opening chapter of the *Qur'an* is read.

(f) The burial of the body.

(g) The mourning following burial.

4. The Muslim idea of what happens to the person who has died in the afterlife is also straightforward. At this point the day of judgment must be mentioned and the events expected on that day must be studied. (Show the sections from the *Qur'an* which describe these expectations.)

5. It is important to stress the following points:

(a) Post-mortem examination is forbidden except in very special circumstances.

(b) Prolonging life by artificial methods is forbidden. (Discuss here the now common practice of using life-support machines, medication etc. to prolong life. Would the Muslim attitude present problems to doctors?)

(c) Muslims should be buried among Muslims in a Muslim cemetery.

(d) A Muslim should preferably be buried at the place of death.

Resources

Sheet 11: Muslim Death Rites.

Books: *Islam*, J. B. Taylor.
   A Muslim Family in Britain, S. W. Harrison & D. Shepherd.
   Life Among Muslims, D. G. Butler.
   The Way of the Muslim, Dr Muhammad Iqbal.

A scheme of work for Sikhism

1. In Sikhism birth (*janam*) and death (*maran*) are always associated. This must be explained. Then a consideration of how Sikhs perceive God must take place if their idea of death is to be fully understood. Death is not seen as the end of life but as the door through which the believer must pass in order to enjoy the full

bliss of God's presence.

2. Consider the Sikh perception of the afterlife. As in other faiths, heaven and hell are seen as states of mind and not geographical localities. Mention belief in reincarnation. Hell is the corrective experience of lower lives which will be suffered as a result of the person's behaviour in previous lives. It is important to note that God has given human beings the freedom to decide whether they prefer heaven, so being with God, or hell. For the Sikh judgment takes place *immediately* after death.

3. At the death ceremony no wailing or outward mourning is encouraged. Bodies are cremated (cf. Islam) and prayers are offered to the deceased. During the ten days following the funeral, the bereaved family will read the Guru Granth Sahib (the Sikhs' holy book) from beginning to end.

Resources

Sheet 12: The Sikh Death Ceremony.

Books: *Life Among Sikhs*, D. G. Butler.
A Sikh Family in Britain, W. Owen Cole.
The Way of the Sikh, W. H. McLeod.

For this unit of work, dealing with religious customs and beliefs, I have not mentioned activities, but I have offered advice on what to include within each scheme. When I study such a topic with my own classes I like to allow them to present their work in project form. In the past they have also carried out visual work, devising informative 'posters' illustrating one or two of each faith's beliefs and customs. This follows on from the project work.

If there are members of faiths other than Christianity in the classroom, then it would be useful to encourage these pupils to talk about their own beliefs and customs concerning death. If possible, a class can be divided into groups and each group allocated a different religion. Then each group can be invited to play the various roles of family, friends, pall-bearers, clergy and so on and act out the death and burial customs. The role-play can be shown to the remainder of the class and a discussion of the etiquette, responsibilities and possible feelings associated with each role should be interesting and rewarding. If this scheme is carried out, it may give pupils a better idea of the different religious customs which are practised. At the end of such a scheme of work it would be interesting to discuss the differences involved in the various religious beliefs concerning death and to ask the pupils to say which they prefer overall and why. (It might be best for this to take place after the humanist and Marxist views have also been studied.)

A useful general resource to help in studying the various religious beliefs would be G. Parrinder's, *Search for Meaning. Something After Death? Landmarks in Life*, by C. Brittain & M. Tredinnick is also good.

Objective: To look at examples of non-religious attitudes to death, through a study of humanism and Marxism

The purpose of this is to present pupils with beliefs and ideas which have arisen from the considerable growth in agnosticism in the last hundred years.

Activities

1. Facts must be given to explain humanist and Marxist beliefs.

2. Sheet 13, 'The Humanist Notion of Death' (appendix three). Read and discuss with pupils any ideas here which are new to them.

3. When discussing Marxist ideas the notion of human struggle and suffering in this life as compensated for in a better society for future generations must be discussed.

4. When these two philosophies have been studied and discussed a comparison may be made between the two and then their ideas can be compared with religious ideas already studied. Ask pupils to consider which notion of death and afterlife they prefer and why.

Resources

  Sheet 13: The Humanist Notion of Death.

  Book: *The Humanist Outlook*, A. J. Ayer.

Objective: To acquaint pupils with the legal and medical definitions of death and with the legalities and problems of body and organ donation

Activities

1. Learn traditional and emerging definitions of death. What is

'brain death'? Consider the ethical issues here and discuss the problems of defining 'brain death'.

2. If possible, using blood-pressure equipment, stethoscope and reflex hammer, allow pupils to find the vital signs of life and reflex action.

3. Learn the legal procedures for the certification of death and show a death certificate.

4. Ask a doctor to talk about the vital signs, and how death is certified. Then discuss the current practices for organ donation (showing examples of donor cards) and how this can affect the family.

5. Further discussion of 'brain death'. Who should decide whether this has occurred? The doctor? The family? Consider the possibility of euthanasia. Show the 'Living Will' and explain the 'exit declaration'. To whom should euthanasia be offered? Point out the differences between compulsory and voluntary euthanasia. *Perspectives,* by M. A. Chignell, contains an excellent summary of the arguments for and against euthanasia.

6. If possible show the film, *Logan's Run*. This is concerned with a life, envisaged in the future, when people are conditioned to accept compulsory euthanasia; the film explores what happens when some people object to this practice.

Resources

    Sheet 15: A 'Living Will'.

    Film: *Logan's Run*.

    Medical equipment.

Objective: To introduce the pupil to a variety of methods of body disposal, current funeral practices and relative costs

Activities

1. If possible, and only with the permission of parents, take the pupils on a visit to a funeral home. It is advisable for the teacher to visit the home first to become familiar with the surroundings and objects. The teacher ought to ensure that there are no bodies present during the class visit.

2. Before the visit the pupils should be made aware of what they will see during their visit. They should already know about religious funeral and burial customs from studying earlier units of work.

3. Before the visit compile a questionnaire and have pupils answer questions relating to funeral practices. At the end of the visit have them answer it once again to see if they can be more explicit in their views.

4. The various methods and costs of body disposal should now be presented:

   (a) Burial.

   (b) Cremation.

   (c) Organ and body donation.

   (d) Cyronics (freezing bodies).

5. Encourage the pupils to talk to parents, grandparents and other family members about funeral customs in their family and then prepare reports to be entered into their books.

Objective: To survey the theories concerning suicide and its occurrence in our culture; to discuss both the moral and religious views and to have pupils explore their own feelings about suicide

Activities

1. Isolate the theme of suicide in poetry and song. Some examples which could be presented to the pupils are 'Save the Life of My Child', P. Simon; 'Vincent', D. McClean; poetry by Sylvia Plath.

2. Discuss what relationship the suicidal thoughts in the songs and poems have to the themes of the songs and poems. Why do the pupils think artists/poets use such a theme? Is there a relationship between the artist's life and suicidal thoughts? (e.g. Sylvia Plath actually committed suicide.)

3. Identify 'famous' suicides in history and the reasons for these suicides. (i.e. Vincent Van Gogh, Ernest Hemingway.)

4. Discuss why adolescents commit suicide. The teacher should

provide information as to why teenagers commit suicide and what counselling services are available (for example, the Samaritans) in the community. Confidentiality must be encouraged.

Resources

Songs and poetry illustrating the theme of suicide.
Durkheim's work on the sociology of suicide, *Suicide*, will be useful to teachers as it provides a convenient summary of the issues of suicide and its causes.

Objective: To inform pupils of the facts of famine and the widespread death it causes

(But note that, as previously mentioned, I would normally study this subject as a separate topic, in its own right.)

Activities

1. Provide pupils with some facts about 'stunted lives'. Discuss what famine is and what its effects are.

2. Pupils produce project work covering the topic. Included in this would be responses to the following 'prompts':
   a) What is famine?
   b) What are the causes of famine?
   c) What are the results of famine?
   d) What can be done to help famine victims?
   e) Give some information on various relief organizations (e.g. Red Cross, Oxfam, VSO) who attempt to help famine victims. Provide some information on how they carry out their relief programmes.

Resources

Books: *Christian Aid*, R. J. Owen.
      Christianity in Action Today, D. D. Pringle.
      How the other Half Dies? S. George (for the teacher's reference).
      Perspectives, M. A. Chignell.
      Who Cares?, F. G. Herod.

TV Programme: 'The Small Miracle' – about São Paulo – shows how poverty can cause disease and death.

Chapter 7
Conclusions

The late medieval woodcuts of the dance of death show people from all walks of life dancing with skeletons as their partners. The motto engraved on these woodcuts is 'Remember, O man, that you shall die'. The message may have been a comforting one, for the prints were very popular. Today it is not a message most of us would want to hear, for we have grown up in a culture in which the reality of death is avoided physically and mentally. Yet the message on the woodcuts is the truth, for we will die, and everyone we love will die or has already died. In interacting with young people about death, we are not encountering an unknown subject; we are dealing with something which is known only too well by us all.

I have attempted to stress the importance of children learning about death and beyonds to death. I have sought to show ways in which, within the framework of religious studies or religious education, teachers can help them to cope with this sensitive topic. We must attempt to help our pupils in their search for truth and, particularly in the technological society of today, to realize that truth cannot be found in a one-sided approach.

Our aim is to introduce the child to the many different aspects of death. We must stress that in addition to the biological and social facts about death, there is our own less conscious awareness of what is happening. We are all, even without actually coming into contact with death, to some degree aware of death and that we will all eventually lose those we love. So it is important for our pupils to come to understand what death is and to be given the chance to come to understand what beliefs people have concerning death. Attention must be given to the wider pattern of belief surrounding ideas to do with death, for these very ideas may have been instrumental in shaping existing doctrines. To familiarize children with these beliefs is to encourage them to come to terms with their own fears and/or questions concerning death. It should help them to realize that they are not alone in wondering about death; it is something which has puzzled and concerned the human race since the beginning of time.

I believe that the whole subject of death merits greater attention in our schools. Some believe it is a subject too personal to be dealt with at school and should be left to parents. I believe it is not a subject which can be learned about only at home. The school can be more objective about the subject. The kinds of resources that are available to the teacher are not always available at home. The child who is presented with the facts and different ways of looking at a particular life problem will probably have more flexibility with which to solve the problem. It would be unwise to ignore the dangers attached to teaching such a sensitive topic; however, to avoid the topic would be unreal. It would certainly require great sensitivity on the part of the teacher, but it would be wrong to believe that we have to be great 'psychological wizards' to teach about death and dying. It would simply be necessary to recognize that personal and professional life interact in all our teaching about death. If we wish to do a better professional job in teaching this subject, because of its emotional impact, we must come to understand our own interactions with it. Once we know our own true feelings, we will be better able to understand what is going on in the feelings and minds of our pupils.

By teaching the subject within religious studies or religious education I would hope to show my pupils that death is a universal experience which has given rise to a great number of beliefs concerning what lies beyond death. I would also want to help them to see that religious involvement is one way of coping with death, and that their own perceptions of such matters are far from trivial even if their ability to reason about them is limited. Merely to teach the facts about death is not enough; both the emotional and spiritual aspects must also be explored in an attempt to help the pupils to find appropriate ways of expressing their own deepest convictions.

I have attempted to explain how teachers can listen and respond to their pupils' own fears and questions, and have included specific goals for 'death education' within religious studies. I have outlined the sorts of activities, readings, and audio-visual aids which can be used to help children confront an especially difficult and important aspect of life.

Appendix One

A Summary of Research by S. Anthony and Others on Children's Developmental Ideas of Death and Their Observed Emotional Responses

Anthony found that very young children, by putting all the things they see together with the language they hear and making no attempt to separate 'what' from 'why' often have very creative theories about death. One of the most common is that death and birth are cycles within the same entity. She found that many children thought that putting a dead body in water would bring it back to life. Others believed the cycle was within a larger cosmic system, so that in order for one person to be born, it was necessary for someone else to die.

In an attempt to discover how children (aged from five to fourteen years) develop in their ability to understand death, Anthony inserted the word 'dead' into the vocabulary scale of a test of general intelligence (the English revision of the Terman-Merrill form of the Binet scale). She then judged the answer on a scale that measured the degree to which the answer approximated to an adult scientific definition rather than an emotional definition occurring in crisis situations. The degrees of knowledge with regard to an understanding of the definition of death were found to fall into five categories:

(a) Apparent ignorance of the word 'dead'.

(b) Interest in the word or fact combined with limited or erroneous concept.

(c) No evidence of non-comprehension of the meaning of 'dead', but definition by reference to (a) associated phenomena not biologically or logically essential, or (b) humanity specifically.

(d) Correct, essential but limited reference.

(e) General, logical, or biological definition or description.

Two-thirds of the children tested answered in the (c) category.

The scale, however, does tend to be related to mental age. No child below mental age 8 answered (a) and (b). No child under five years of age answered (c), (d), and (e). (S. Anthony, *The Discovery of Death in Childhood and After*, p. 49.)

The two-thirds of the answers given in the (c) category include such definitions of 'dead' as 'when you're in your coffin', and 'something that's been killed', and, 'when you go to heaven if you've been good'. As Anthony shows, by defining the category in the negative, the children's answers clearly indicate that the children know what death is. They are not able to construct an abstract definition but fall back instead upon concrete examples of death within their experience or imagination. The (d) category has the example, 'when you are dead you can't come alive again', and in the (e) category death is 'a body that has no life in it'. These two categories are advanced but show no more knowledge of what death is; they only show a greater ability to form abstract thoughts.

A majority of children of primary school age gave answers in the (c) category. The creative answers given in categories (a) and b) are not innately wrong ideas but are logical thoughts based on their information and experience at their level of cognition. Death, at this stage, is a subject of intellectual inquiry and interest as early as three years of age. At this age, the child's answers are based on common sense, observable information, and fantasy. The following examples are taken from *The Discovery of Death*:

> A2 (Reported by a school teacher) Marlene (2:11) was brought to school by her father, who had found her lying asleep by her dead mother on the floor by a half-made bed. The mother had suffered a heart-attack. On arrival at school, Marlene said quite happily to the teacher, 'Mother lay down on the floor and went to sleep, so I went to sleep too' (pp. 50–51).

After five years of age, the child gave answers based on information gained from adults. For example,

> B4 Stephen (4:10) quite frequently comes up against it (death) and puzzles for a few minutes. . . . At present he thinks that we all turn into statues when we die, owing to the fact that he met Queen Victoria as a statue in Kensington

Gardens and then was told that she had been dead for some time. The dead birds in poultry shops obviously puzzle him, and at first he thought they were asleep (p. 52).

Does this mean that children of this age could understand the concept of death if the teaching were presented factually?

Maria Nagy's work (1948) forms a kind of transition between intellectual understanding and emotional response. She asked 378 children between three and ten years old to tell her whatever came into their minds on the subject of death. Older children wrote and some younger children drew pictures. She found three stages. In the first stage, up to five years, children do not see death as final. Rather, death is a departure or is seen as reversible like sleep and is not separated from life. They think the dead can still eat, talk, and so on; it is just that they do it under the ground, or in heaven. The most frightening idea that death represents for very young children is separation from the maternal influence in their lives.

Nagy's second stage is from about the age of five through to nine years. Death is understood as final but is personified as a 'bogeyman', a skeleton, a reaper or some other common pictoral representation of death. Nagy says the third stage begins after nine years and is essentially like adult ideas about death.

There are some highly speculative theories about children and death. One of the most speculative is that infants have a fear of nonbeing which becomes the fear of death when they are old enough to conceptualize. Adah Maurer believes that the game 'peek-a-boo' is a way in which the young child masters the innate fear of nonbeing which is brought on by breaks in the child's perception of the mother's presence, such as when the child sleeps or cries for the absent mother. She says that the phrase 'peek-a-boo' comes from an Old English phrase meaning 'life or death'. In playing the game, the child comes to be in charge of who is there and who is not. However, it must be remembered that this theory is purely speculative.

It is Anthony who has given us the most significant clues to childhood fears of death. In *The Discovery of Death* (p. 79) she describes how she gave children (aged five to fourteen years) open-ended stories and asked them to complete them. She found that the majority of references to death came from these story openings:

> One Sunday the boy (or they all) went out for the day with his (their) father and mother. When they came home in the evening, the mother was very sad. Why?

> One night he cried when he went to bed; he was very unhappy. Why was that?

> He woke up again in the middle of the night, and was very frightened. Why?

She found that there were two sorts of responses to these story openings: sorrow and fear. Sorrow came from fears of separation from a parent, although in the first opening, the sorrow originates from the mother's sadness because of the death of the father. Fear occurs in the context of violent aggression. The children associated death with a violent external source, either from outside the home – like a burglar – or inside the home – like a ghost. This last finding is very much like Nagy's stage in which the child personified and externalized death as an aggressive enemy.

Some studies of older children have shown that fear and thoughts of death have helped us to understand other aspects of adolescents' lives. It seems that bright, emotionally mature adolescents can deal with thoughts of death better than those who have problems in other areas of their lives. Maurer asked 172 schoolgirls to write an essay on, 'What comes into your mind when you think about death? She then grouped the essays by the number of fear words used and correlated that with the level of academic achievement. She found that poor achievers had a greater fear of death, showing separation anxiety and remnants of beliefs in ghosts (Nagy's second stage) as well as a preoccupation with disease and violence. Low achievers often mentioned physical things like the smell of corpses. The less able girls were more likely to be overtly afraid of death, expressing thoughts and feelings about life and death more often than the normal population.

Appendix Two

A Review of Research on Children's Understanding of Death

There are many studies devoted to children's understanding of death. It is the purpose of this appendix to review some of these in the hope that they will prove to be of help to people who may find themselves in a pastoral role when teaching children about death, and helping to further their understanding of death, and helping to eradicate any fears of death. There is considerable evidence to show that an understanding of death is a developmental feature of human intelligence, and that its genesis is very early; this would need to be taken into consideration when teaching about death. Lesson content must match the child's level of cognitive development if a proper understanding is to be reached.

KOOCHER, G. P., *Childhood, Death and Cognitive Development*, **1973**

This study focuses on three levels of cognitive functioning:

    i)   the pre-operational sub-period.

    ii) the concrete-operational sub-period.

    iii) the formal-operational period as described by Piaget.

Using Piaget's framework for conceptualizing cognitive development, children's attitudes toward death were explored and analysed.

The Sample
Koocher tested a group of seventy-five children, from six to fifteen years of age, and with average intellectual ability. They were tested to determine primary level of cognitive functioning and then asked four questions:

    i)   What makes things die?

    ii) How can you make dead things come to life?

    iii) When will you die?

    iv) What happens then?

Results

Replies to these questions were shown to be related to the child's level of cognitive development. Not a single child in the study gave a personification-type response when asked what would happen at the time of death. This lack of personification reflects cultural differences but also suggests a different sort of coping mechanism from the one Nagy found in her sample. She noted in her article, 'The Child's Theories Concerning Death', that Hungarian children between five and nine generally personified death. She wrote that children will keep death at a distance in this way, because 'only those die whom the death man carry off' (p. 26).

Koocher found in his study that even children who were capable of above average levels of verbal abstraction were consistently specific and concrete in their answers. Their concreteness may, he feels, reflect either a lack of experience with death as compared with other worldly phenomena, or perhaps a defence against the uncertainties of death to the child. Children of middle-class midwestern background, of average intelligence, Koocher suggests, are inclined to use specificity of detail rather than personification as a means to mastery and hence 'control' over death. 'If I know exactly what is going to happen when I die, then I have no need to worry about it now.' If it is as Koocher suggests, then the importance of explaining death to children is paramount.

WILLIAMS, R. L. and COLE, S., *Religiosity, Generalized Anxiety and Apprehension Concerning Death*, 1968

Freud affirmed that above all else the prospect of death impels human beings to fabricate divine beings to protect themselves from the ultimate threat of nature. Religion therefore, was considered to be a prime symptom of neurosis and a product of paranoid minds. If one accepted Freud's view one would expect both prevailing insecurity and preoccupation with death to be characteristic of the highly religious. Williams and Cole, in this study, set out to contradict this.

The Sample

The subjects were taken from introductory psychology classes at a state college in the Southern States of America. 161 students were chosen – 29 of high religiosity, 21 of intermediate religiosity, and 24 of low religiosity.

They were asked to indicate the extent of their church attendance, personal prayer, reading of religious material, Sunday School attendance and church-related activity. They were then subjected to various tests to discover their level of insecurity and their thoughts on death.

Results

These were divided into two segments: generalized insecurity indices and death-related insecurity. It was shown that the high and intermediate religiosity groups did not differ in security levels, but that both were significantly more secure than the low religiosity group. Williams and Cold believed that their investigation failed to produce any support for the hypothesized Freudian relationship between religion and neurotic inclinations. On all dimensions of anxiety, the active religious subjects manifested the highest level of adjustment. From their study they concluded that the high religiosity group manifested the least anxiety on all dimensions, including their attitude to death, and the low religiosity group the greatest generalized insecurity.

MAURER, A., *The Child's Knowledge of Non-Existence*, 1961

Maurer believes that there is considerable evidence to show that an understanding of death is a developmental feature of human intelligence, and that its genesis is very early. She points out that Nagy's study (see appendix one) leaves no doubt that children are very concerned with the problem of death. Both her study and some carried out afterwards seem to point to the fact that children fear death and their answers to questions asked seemed to bear a relation to their age. Maurer believes that to leave a child to cope with its fear will lead to psychological problems.

She quotes Bertrand Russell to show how she feels the problem can be dealt with successfully: 'The idea that falsehood is edifying is one of the besetting sins of those who draw up educational schemes. . . . The kind of virtue that can be produced by guarded ignorance is frail and fails at first touch of reality. . . . It is thought that the knowledge of things as they are will lead to cynicism, and so it may if knowledge comes suddenly with a shock of surprise and horror.'

In view of this she feels that the subject of death is not one which should be avoided with children, however young they may be. To withhold information about death, or to give false information, especially when a child shows curiosity, may well cause children to come to fear it.

The results from research undertaken with children seem to point to the fact that thoughts of death are frequent in children. Children appear to deal realistically with death; they are ready to believe that others can die, but do not regard their own deaths as probable. Research suggests that the child's fear can be dealt with if death is spoken of openly and if it is not avoided as a topic of conversation.

There also seems to be reasonable agreement in these studies that the child's thinking about death is a progressive feature of human intelligence. Therefore, when teaching about death the child's level of cognitive development must be taken into account and it must be dealt with sensitively. When discussing death each child's reaction should be noted carefully and if any distress is shown it must be dealt with immediately and carefully.

I would therefore suggest that the religious studies teacher who decides to teach about death must regard the subject as one for serious consideration. Various studies have shown that the child wishes to be safe in death. So a discussion of death and beyonds to death would be an invaluable addition to any school syllabus, aiming to help further the child's understanding of a difficult subject.

Appendix Three

1. Voices

1. I don't really remember what it was like being young. I never thought about death much. Then I had a stroke and I'm nearly crippled. People come to see me and help me, but I feel like a burden. I get cold in the morning, very cold. I don't move around easily. My body isn't strong; it's worse at night. I don't sleep. I've no wife, no family, but I choose to live like this – I try to be as independent as I can. My friends are nearly all dead, or like me.

2. When I was younger this used to be a lovely area. It was happier then. People were more helpful. Now it's poor and rough. Sometimes I daren't go out. I can't afford to move. I'm frightened about what will happen to me. What if I'm ill? What if I die? I only hope it's quick. It's all got to end some time. I like to think there's a heaven; it's a comfort to think that.

3. I'm old and I'm dying. I used to be afraid of death, when I had something to live for, but not now. I suppose I've got to make way for the younger ones. If there is something after, good, if not . . . well, I won't know about it, will I?

4. When I was younger I never thought much about death, I just got on with living. Now, since my husband died, I think about it more. I hope I see my husband again, but I don't know.

5. Young people don't know. They think we're nuisances, senile. They don't realize we were young as well. They laugh, but they'll be old too. I look old, but inside I'm young – I just don't act young. I'd like to do all sorts of things now – but I know my time's running out. Kids don't know how lucky they are. When I was young, it never bothered me. Now I think of all that time gone, all gone.

6. Fourteen years ago my husband died and then my two sons married. Suddenly, I was alone and living in a house full of happy memories. So I sold the house and moved into a flat near one of my sons. I even took a course at evening classes, I wasn't too

lonely. But then I had to give it up. I was finding it hard to move around without help. Now I began to know what loneliness was like. I just sat and watched the television. I would look at my old photos to try to relive the happy days. My sons don't visit me too often. There's a day centre just opened near me, I go when it's open. It's the only thing I've got to look forward to; I still get lonely though. Only people who've been lonely can really understand what it means. Death – well it frightens me sometimes and then I think, so what! Nobody will miss me. I suppose I'm just waiting for my turn now.

2. A Crabbit Old Woman Wrote This

What do you see nurses, what do you see?
Are you thinking when you look at me –
A crabbit old woman, not very wise,
Uncertain of habit, with far away eye,
Who dribbles her food, and makes no reply
When you say in a loud voice, 'I do wish you'd try!'
Who seems not to notice the things that you do,
And forever is losing a stocking or shoe.
Who, unresisting or not, lets you do as you will,
With bathing and feeding, the long day to fill.
Is that what you are thinking? Is that what you see?
Then open your eyes, nurse, you're looking at me.
I tell you who I am as I sit here so still,
As I use at your bidding, as I eat at your will,
I'm a small child often with a father and mother,
Brothers and sisters who love one another.
A young girl of sixteen, with wings on her feet,
Dreaming that soon now a lover she'll meet.
A bride soon a-twenty, my heart gives a leap,
Remembering the vows that I promised to keep;
At twenty-five now I have young of my own,
Who need me to build a secure, happy home;
A woman of thirty, my young now grow fast,
Bound to each other with ties that should last.
At forty, my young sons have grown and gone,
But my man's beside me to see I don't mourn.
At fifty, once more babies play round my knee,
Again we know children, my loved one and me.
Dark days are upon me, my husband is dead,
I look to the future, I shudder with dread,
For my young are all rearing young of their own,
And I think of the years and the love that I've known.
I'm now an old woman and nature is cruel –
'Tis jest to make old age look like a fool.

The body it crumbles, grace and vigour depart,
There now is a stone where I once had a heart.
But inside this old carcass a young girl still dwells,
And now and again my battered heart swells,
I remember the joys, I remember the pain,
And I'm loving and living life over again.
I think of the years all too few gone too fast,
And accept the stark fact that nothing can last.
So open your eyes, nurses, open and see,
Not a crabbit old woman, look closer.

See me!

(Anonymous)

3. Children's Experiences of Death

1. Child: But what means dead, mummy?

Mother: Well, your heart stops beating and you lie still without breathing.

Child: And what do you do with the talking part – you know the inside talk?

Mother: I'm not sure, but some people think you live in another world, and, of course, some don't.

Child: I guess we do (excitedly). Yes! And then you die in a long, long time – a very long time, and then I die and we both hug each other and then you won't have any wrinkles – Oh, look at that cute pussy. Isn't she a darling? (Runs off) (V. Madge, *Children in Search of Meaning*, p. 16).

2. That Christmas was the loneliest I had ever spent. . . . Dad spent all day in Roynton with grandpa. Mum tried to keep me happy, but for those last few weeks I had been well prepared for the worst. . . . It was very late when I went to bed, but dad had not returned . . . grandpa had died during the night. I felt a horrible ache in my throat . . . tears were welling up in my eyes. . . . I get that same feeling every time I look back on that strange night (D. C. Measham, *Fourteen: Autobiography of an Age-Group*).

3. *Our Baby Died*

A year ago, our baby died
He died committing suicide,
Some say he died to spite us, of spinal meningitis
'Twas a nasty baby anyhow and cost us 40 dollars,
And only lived 3 hours.
We didn't send it any flowers,
'Cos it wasn't ours. (*Songfest*, (eds) D. and B. Best).

4. Prayers Recited at the Hindu Funeral Ceremony

Thou art the Primal God, Ancient Being; Thou art the Final Resting Place of this Universe, Thou art the Knower, the Knowledge and the Supreme Abode; by Thee is the Universe pervaded, and Thy form is infinite.

When one layeth his worn out robes away and takes new ones, so the spirit casts away the old body and takes a new one.

For certain is the death of the born, and certain is the birth of the dead; therefore grieve not for what is inevitable (The Gita).

I know the Supreme Absolute Being who is full of splendour like the sun far beyond the darkness of ignorance. By knowing Him alone can one conquer death and attain eternal bliss. There is no other path for the attainment of Salvation! (Yajur Veda).

May your eyesight return to the sun, your breath to the winds; may your water mingle with the ocean and your earthly part become one with the earth. The indestructible spirit passes on into another body according to the actions performed in this life (Atharva Veda).

Oh Mortal, by the austerity and enlightenment, and by thy good deeds, attain bliss in heaven and join the Company of thy forbears. Be free from all sins and once again may thy Spirit inherit an enlightened body full of lustre. And once again mayest thou come to this world to perform noble deeds (Rig Veda).

The Spirit which is immortal is not made of the five elements and cannot perish. This body will be reduced to ashes and dust. Therefore, O Mortal, remember Om, and with him thy past deeds, the deeds you are doing, as by so doing one can attain salvation (Isho Upanishad).

5. The Hindu Attitude to the Soul

As a man leaves an old garment and puts on one that is new, the spirit leaves his mortal body, and wanders on to one that is new.

Weapons cannot hurt the spirit, and fire can never burn him. Untouched is he by drenching waters. Untouched is he by parching winds.

Invisible before birth are all beings, and after death invisible again. They are seen between two unseens – why in this truth find sorrow? (Bhagavad Gita, Chapter 2).

6. The Hindu Attitude to Life

Everything perishes with the death of the body. It is only *dharma* that is our best friend, which even after death remains with the Spirit. Therefore do not allow *dharma* to perish, for perished *dharma* brings about our own destruction (Manusmriti).

7. Mourning in Judaism

Close relatives of the deceased – spouse, parents, children, brothers and sisters – are considered mourners. Comforting the mourner (*nihum avelim*) is regarded in Judaism as one of the primary social duties. There are four periods of mourning:

(a) From death until burial. During this period the mourner is known as an *onen*. He/she should spend this time making preparations for the funeral; the *onanium* (plural) are exempt from certain religious obligations (e.g. regular prayer). During this time the mourner is not comforted: 'Rabbi Simeon ben Eleazar said: "do not comfort your fellow while his dead lies before him"' (Mishnah Avot 4.23).

At the commencement of the funeral the mourners tear one of their garments – this act of mourning is known as *kriah* (tearing).

(b) The *shiva*: For seven days after the funeral, the close relatives gather daily at the house of mourning. They sit on low chairs, and family, friends and neighbours come to offer them comfort and condolence. Daily prayers, including special prayers in memory of the deceased are said. During the period of the *shiva* (literally 'seven') deep mourning is observed. The mourners may not shave, have their hair cut, go to work, or prepare food for themselves.

(c) *Shaloshim*: For a further three weeks (until *shaloshim*, thirty days after the funeral) personal mourning is observed. The mourner may go to work, but should avoid, if possible, shaving and haircuts; no new clothes may be worn, nor may the mourner listen to any music or take part in any celebration.

Mourners have the privilege of reciting a particular piece of the liturgy – the *kaddish* (see below) – at all public prayers that they attend. Most Jewish people see the observance of this privilege as a duty – and will make every effort to attend synagogue services during their period of mourning.

(d) From *shaloshim* to first *Yahzeit*: The full period of mourning, observed for parents and children, is one year from the date of death. *Kaddish* is said for eleven months, and during this time the *avelim* (mourners) still observe certain patterns of mourning. The tombstone may be erected and consecrated at any time from the end of the *shaloshim*, but not normally later than the first *Yahzeit* (anniversary of death, from the Yiddish). Each year the *Yahzeit* is marked by reciting *kaddish*, lighting a memorial candle and performing some righteous act.

Kaddish

This prayer is one of the best known parts of the Jewish liturgy. Although originally used for different purposes one variant of it (the *Mourners' Kaddish*) has for centuries been used exclusively for recitation by mourners in the synagogue. It is said in its original language, Aramaic. It is neither a prayer for the dead nor to the dead, but a powerful assertion by a mourner who has encountered death at close quarters of faith in the Creator, ending with a plea for peace.

Note: I have described traditional Jewish belief and practice as it is still observed by the Orthodox Jewish community. The Reform and Liberal Jewish communities have amended the rituals of mourning in a number of ways – for example, cremation is permitted, *shiva* is not necessarily observed for the full period; *kriah* is not observed. However, the basic principles and belief as outlined above are common to all sections of the Jewish community.

8. *The Buddhist Funeral Service*

At a funeral, the coffin is brought into the crematorium chapel and a photograph of the deceased is placed upon or beside the coffin to remind the congregation of the transient nature of life.

A monk who has been invited to conduct the funeral service leads the congregation of Buddhists in the traditional dedications of respect for their Teacher. These are recited in Pali, the ancient language of Buddhist scripture, each section being repeated three times:

> Exaltation to the Blessed One, saint and perfectly Enlightened One.
> I go for refuge to the Buddha.
> I go for refuge to the *Dhamma* (his Teaching).
> I go for refuge to the *Sangha* (the order of Enlightened Disciples).

Next the congregation repeats to the monk the Five Precepts – guidelines and commitments to the moral life. These are voluntary and undertaken freely by each individual as a code of inner spiritual development as well as of action:

> I undertake to maintain the Precept to abstain from harming life.
> I undertake to maintain the Precept to abstain from taking what is not given.
> I undertake to maintain the Precept to abstain from sensual impropriety.
> I undertake to maintain the Precept to abstain from unskilful speech.
> I undertake to maintain the Precept to abstain from taking intoxicants which cause heedlessness.

The monk recites a verse in canonical language which bears the following meaning:

All conditioned things are transient;
Their nature is to arise and to pass away;
They are born and they die;
The cessation of conditioned things is liberation.

To symbolize the transference of pure thoughts (merits) to the departed, the next of kin or a friend pours water from a vessel to an empty bowl until it overflows into a dish below, while reciting the following lines:

Let the pure thoughts of goodwill be shared by my relative and
    may he (she) be happy.
As water runs from rivers to fill the ocean,
So may well-being and merit within us
Pour forth and reach our beloved departed one,
Who may thus be filled therewith,
And share these thoughts with us.

There follows then a sermon on the subject of impermanence. The purpose of the sermon is to bring the mourners to a calm and mature understanding of the universal phenomenon of death, and to realize this in sympathy together. At this time, it is told how the Buddha dealt with the grief of the young mother, Kisagetami, when she visited him, distraught at the death of her two-year old son who had suddenly been struck down as he played.

Taking the corpse of the boy upon her hip, Kisagetami went, crazed with sorrow, from door to door, saying, 'Give me medicine for my son.' And people said with contempt, 'Medicine? What is the use? You are man.' But she understood them not, and walked on till she came to the Buddha. 'Exalted One,' she said, 'Give me medicine for my child, that he may become well again.' And the Buddha, seeing her condition, said, 'Go enter the town and at any house where yet no one has died, thence bring me some mustard seed.' 'It is well, Lord,' she said, and hurried away on her quest.

Wherever she went the people were ready to give her as much mustard seed as she wanted, but when she told them of the condition laid down by the Buddha, no one could help her, for death had been everywhere at some time or other and taken his toll. And even as the Master had foreseen, Kisagetami realized the inevitability of death and, taking her child to the graveyard, had the funeral ceremonies performed, saying aloud that all may heed:

No village law is this, no city law,
No law for this clan alone, no law for that one.
For the whole world, ahe, and the gods in high heaven,
This is the law – all is impermanent, all must die.

9. The Christian Funeral Service

The funeral is a ceremony performed before the body is buried or cremated. When there is a church funeral, the funeral director brings the body to the church (or chapel) in a hearse. At the church the hearse is met by the priest or clergyman who is going to read the burial service. In Catholic churches there may be a service called a Requiem Mass. This is a special service of Holy Communion at which prayers are said for the deceased.

In all church funerals, prayers are said when the body has been taken from the church building, and is being placed in the ground. Here is an extract from the Church of England's 1662 service:

> When they come to the grave, while the corpse is made ready to be laid into the earth, the priest shall say, or the priest and clerks shall sing:

> Man that is born of a woman hath but a short time to live, and is full of misery. He cometh up, and is cut down like a flower: he fleeth as it were a shadow, and never continueth in one stay.

> In the midst of life we are in death: of whom may we seek for succour, but of thee, O Lord, who for our sins are justly displeased?

> Then while the earth shall be cast upon the body by some standing by, the priest shall say,

> Forasmuch as it hath pleased Almighty God of his great, mercy to take unto himself the soul of our dear brother (sister) here departed, we therefore commit his (her) body to the ground; earth to earth, ashes to ashes, dust to dust; in sure and certain hope of the Resurrection to eternal life, through our Lord Jesus Christ . . .

Lord, have mercy upon us.
Christ have mercy upon us.
Lord have mercy upon us.

The Catholic service is slightly different. At the graveside the priest sprinkles the grave and the body with holy water and incenses them. As the body is lowered into the grave, or at any other suitable time, the priest may say:

It has pleased Almighty God to call our brother (sister) from this life to Himself. Accordingly we commit his (her) body to the earth whence it came. Since Christ, the first fruits of the dead, has risen again and will refashion our frail body in the pattern of his glorious risen body, we commend our brother (sister) to the Lord. May He embrace him (her) in his peace and bring his (her) body to life again on the last day.

Although the words spoken at these funeral services may differ the intention is the same – to commit the dead person into the care of God, and to pray for those who mourn.

Cremation

The service is similar to that of the burial service except that the body is burned. The whole service may take place at a crematorium. This is a dual-purpose building, consisting of a chapel where the funeral service takes place, and the ovens in which the body is cremated.

The ashes of the deceased are collected and placed in a small box or urn which may then be buried in the cemetery surrounding the crematorium or in the churchyard. Sometimes the ashes are scattered over a lawn in the cemetery or in a place of the deceased's choice. A memorial plaque is usually put up.

10. The Methodist Tradition

The service has a basic structure, but also a number of variations introduced in the Methodist Service Book by the words, 'The Minister may say. . . .' It is therefore flexible enough for use in a variety of circumstances, yet easily recognized as the same service on all occasions. Special variations can be used, for example at the burial of a child, at the minister's discretion.

The Service

The minister, meeting the body and going before it, says one or more of the following sentences:

'I am the resurrection and the life,' says the Lord; 'he who believes in me, though he (she) die, yet shall he (she) live, and whoever lives and believes in me shall not die eternally.'

Blessed are those who mourn, for they shall be comforted.

God so loved the world that he gave his only son, that whoever believes in him should not perish but have eternal life.

Because I live, you will live also.

Once in the church or chapel hymns are sung, the Bible is read and prayers may be said for the deceased and the bereaved.

At the Graveside

The minister, going before the body to the grave, or at the crematorium, will say some of the following:

As a father pities his children, so the Lord pities those who fear him. For he knows our frame; he remembers that we are dust.

The Lord is good to all, and his compassion is over all that he has made. . . .

To this end Christ died and lived again, that he may be Lord of both the dead and of the living.

When the body is laid in the earth or on the catafalque, the minister then says:

Forasmuch as our brother (sister) has departed out of this life and Almighty God in his great mercy has called him (her) to himself, we therefore commit his (her) body to the ground, earth to earth, ashes to ashes, dust to dust (OR, to the elements, ashes to ashes, dust to dust), in sure and certain hope of the resurrection to eternal life through our Lord Jesus Christ, to whom be glory for ever and ever. Amen.

Other prayers can be spoken or additional readings can be added before the service is brought to an end.

11. Muslim Death Rites

Muslims believe that when a person dies his or her soul is taken into the charge of the angel of death to await the resurrection and the last judgment. The soul thus leaves the material world and enters into a 'waiting state' known as *barzakh*. To the soul, this time of waiting will be seen to be just one day. On the day of judgment there will be a cosmic upheaval, and the earth and heavens will be destroyed. Each soul will then be judged according to its deeds while upon earth. Those whose good deeds outweigh the bad will go to paradise, which is pictured as a pleasant garden where the blessed can enjoy rich food and clothing and are served celestial wine. The evil, on the other hand, are thrown into the fire, where they are given hot water to drink and bitter fruit to eat. Both heaven and hell are seen as everlasting, and all souls are sent to one or the other; there is no intermediate state.

When a Muslim is dying, relatives and friends sit round the death-bed reading verses from the *Qur'an* (the Muslim holy book) and praying for the peaceful departure of the soul. If the sick person can do so, he or she should make a final declaration of faith by saying: 'There is no God except Allah, Muhammad is Allah's messenger.' This declaration is called the *shahadah* and is a very important part of the framework of Muslim spiritual life. By saying this before death it is hoped that God will accept the person's life as a Muslim and forgive his or her sins.

The body should be buried as soon as possible, preferably on the day after death. It is prepared for burial by a ritual washing, known as *ghusl*, and is then perfumed and wrapped in a shroud in the form of three pieces of white cotton cloth. In Britain the law requires burial in a coffin but in many Muslim countries coffins are not used. The body is taken either to a mosque or directly to the burial ground, where the funeral prayer, called the *Salatul Janazah*, is read. It includes a prayer asking God's forgiveness for the deceased. The body is buried with the face towards Mecca, the holy city for Muslims and the focal point toward which all

Muslims turn for prayer. The grave itself should be raised a little above the ground to prevent people from walking on it, but high gravestones and monuments are fobidden.

Although it is accepted that mourning for the dead is a natural reaction, exaggerated displays of grief are not allowed. In Islam people mourn by reciting from the *Qur'an* and offering prayers for the dead and in this way are comforted and supported by their faith in a time of grief. The period of mourning which follows the funeral may vary from seven days to three months, during which time relatives of the deceased are not allowed to hold weddings or other celebratory events.

12. The Sikh Death Ceremony

(a) At the death-bed of a Sikh, the relations and friends console themselves and the departing soul by reading *Sukhmani*, the Psalm of Peace.

(b) When death occurs, no loud lamentations are allowed. Instead, the Sikhs exclaim, '*Wahiguru, Wahiguru!*' (Wonderful Lord!)

(c) All dead bodies, whether those of children or grown-up people, are cremated. Where cremation is not possible, it is permissible to throw the dead body into the sea or a river.

(d) The dead body is washed and clothed (complete with all the five symbols) before it is taken out on a bier to the cremation-ground. The procession starts after a prayer and sings suitable hymns on the way. At the cremation-ground the body is placed on the pyre and the nearest relations light the fire. When the fire is fully ablaze, someone reads *Sohila* and offers prayers for the benefit of the dead. Then the people come away, and leave the relations of the dead at their door, where they are thanked and dismissed.

The bereaved family, for the comfort of their own souls as well as for the peace of the departed, start a reading of the Holy Book which may be at their own house or at a neighbouring *gurdwara*. Friends and relations take part in it, and after ten days they again come together when the reading is finished. The usual prayer is offered and *Karah Parshad* distributed.

(e) The charred bones of the dead together with the ashes are taken from the cremation-ground and thrown into the nearest river.

88

(f) It is forbidden to erect monuments over the remains of the dead, although monuments in their honour at any other place would be quite permissible.

Sections (a) to (f) are taken from *Sikhism, Its Ideals and Institutions*, Principal Teja Singh, pp. 109–110.

The following hymn is usually recited during the funeral procession:

Sohi Ravidas

The dawn of a new day
Is the herald of a sunset,
Earth is not thy permanent home.
Life is like a shadow on the wall.
All thy friends have departed,
Thou too must go.
Thou believeth as if life
Were everlasting and endless,
The journey may be long,
Death is ever hovering over us.
Why art thou asleep?
Wake up, O simpleton.
He who gave thee life,
Gives sustenance also,
He is the soul of creation,
He is the all-feeder,
Relinquish me and mine and worship Him
Within thy heart in the morning
Repeat His name.

13. The Humanist Notion of Death

Humanists assume that death is the end of personal existence because personality is seen to disintegrate with the onset of physical disintegration. The onus is on those who believe that personal existence is independent of physical existence to justify their faith.

In the humanist tradition, the Epicureans made a special point of their teaching on death because of the superstitious fears of death then rampant.

A right understanding that death is nothing to us makes the mortality of life enjoyable not by adding to life an illimitable time, but by taking away the yearning after immortality. For life has no terrors for him who has thoroughly apprehended that there are no terrors for him in ceasing to live (*To Menoeceus*, 125).

True to his teaching, on his death-bed Epicurus wrote to a friend:

On this truly happy day of my life, as I am at the point of death, I write this to you. The disease in my bladder and stomach are pursuing their course, lacking nothing of their natural severity; but against all this is the joy in my heart at the recollection of my conversation with you.

Scattered about the Mediterranean lands during the three centuries before Christ were Epicurean epitaphs: *Non fui, fui, non sum, non curo* (I was not, I have been, I am not, I do not mind). The Epicureans did not celebrate funeral rites. They deprecated and sought to eliminate the craving for immortality in any form (fame, for example) as a source of anxiety and disturbance. They regarded it as unnecessary, and destructive of the proper valuation and enjoyment of mortal life, which is available to those who govern their lives by wise choices and the avoidance of excess.

Far from being negative, this attitude is rooted in taking the temporal conditions of all things seriously, as indeed the medium of all existence, the source and condition of all we hold precious. Not to take temporality as seriously as this is in effect contempt for life.

Humanism is creative activity or nothing, and the difference that is made by what anyone does and is need not be recognized and attributed to be real and satisfying. One can be content to remain unknown so long as one is at work as a contributing influence to the making of human life, with consequences that persist.

The death of those near and dear is of course a cause of suffering. Bereavement may be one of the hardest blows of fate. The end of an unfulfilled life is especially hard to accept. But neither the tragedy of wasted talent or misspent time nor the triviality of feeble living spoils the picture of what can be and is achieved within the human span of life.

Ceremonies may help the bereaved to take final leave of a physical presence, but respect for the dead asks more than this. The dead are weak, and their claim lies in the hands of those they leave. Like the Epicureans, modern humanists should not make much of funeral rites, disposal of the body, attendance on it at the tomb; rather, they should encourage friends and relatives to come together to contribute from their memories and impressions to the creation of a new image of the person they knew, harvesting what was cultivated and produced in life. In this posthumous context, the dead live on, not immortal but as an influence still at work in the lives they shared. Neglect of the dead was an ancient impiety. In modern times failure to tend a grave would not be regarded as seriously as the lightness that forgets those who have gone as if they had not been.

CERTIFIED COPY of an ENTRY OF DEATH

Issued at a fee of one shilling in pursuance of the First Schedule to the INDUSTRIAL ASSURANCE AND FRIENDLY SOCIETIES ACT, 1948.

Registration District ....

DEATH in the Sub-district of .... in the ....

No.	1. When and where died	2. Name and surname	3. Sex	4. Age	5. Occupation	6. Cause of death	7. Signature, description, and residence of informant	8. When registered	9. Signature of registrar
48	Doxtord March 1961 General Hospital Sunderland	Mary Elizabeth Teasdale	Female	86	of 14 Nelson Street Sunderland. Widow of William Teasdale a Roiler A Riviter Shipyard	1a. Congestive heart failure 1b. Ith. Bronchitis and Emphysema c. and Bronchopneumonia 11. Hypertensive heart disease Arteriosclerosis Certified by P.P. D Singh	E. Teasdale Son 60. Morley Grove Sunderland	March 1961	J.R. Carlton Registrar

I HEREBY CERTIFY that the above is a true copy of an entry of death in a Register Book in my custody.

Witness my hand this .... day of ...... 18 MAR 1961 ...... 195 . ... Registrar.

Person to whom issued :
Name and surname (in full) ...... Lily Taylor Baker ....
Address ...... 31, Ravenswood Square, Sunderland. ....

Relationship to deceased : child, adopted-child, step-child, grandchild. (Delete those inapplicable.)

CAUTION:—Any person who (1) falsifies any of the particulars on this certificate, or (2) uses a falsified certificate as true, knowing it to be false, is liable to prosecution.

15. A 'Living Will'

Death is as much a reality as birth, growth, maturity and old age – it is the one certainty of life. If the time comes when I, ..., can no longer take part in decisions for my own future, let this statement stand as an expression of my wishes, while I am still of sound mind.

If the situation should arise in which there is no reasonable expectation of my recovery from physical or mental disability, I request that I be allowed to die and not be kept alive by artificial means or 'heroic measures'. I do not fear death itself as much as the indignities of deterioration, dependence and hopeless pain. I therefore ask that medication be mercifully administered to me to alleviate suffering even 'though this may hasten the moment of death.

This request is made after careful consideration. I hope you who care for me will feel morally bound to follow its mandate. I recognize that this appears to place a heavy responsibility upon you, but it is with the intention of relieving you of such responsibility and of placing it upon myself in accordance with my strong convictions, that this statement is made.

Signed . . . .

Date . . . .
Witness . . . .
Witness . . . .

Copies of this request have been given to . . . .
. . . .
. . . .
. . . .

Bibliography

Bibliography

Books

Anderson, R. S., *Theology, Death and Dying*, Blackwell 1986

Anthony, S., *The Discovery of Death in Childhood and After*, Allen Lane 1971

Aries, P., *Western Attitudes to Death: From the Middle Ages to the Present*, Calder and Boyars 1974

Ayer, A. J., *The Humanist Outlook*, Pemberton 1968

Ball, M., *Death*, OUP 1976

Barnett, V., *A Jewish Family in Britain*, Religious and Moral Education Press 1983

Best, D. and B. (eds), *Songfest*, Crown Publishers, New York 1948

Bowker, J., *The Sense of God*, OUP 1973

Bridger, P., *A Hindu Family in Britain*, Religious Education Press 1979

Brittain, C. and Treddinick, M. G., *Landmarks in Life*, Blackie 1985

Burland, C. A., *The Way of the Buddha*, Hulton Educational 1972

Butler, D. G., *Life Among Hindus*, Edward Arnold 1980

Butler, D. G., *Life Among Muslims*, Edward Arnold 1980

Butler, D. G., *Life Among Sikhs*, Edward Arnold 1980

Casson, J. H., *Dying: The Greatest Adventure of My Life*, Christian Medical Fellowship 1980

Chignell, M. A., *Perspectives*, Edward Arnold 1981

Cole, W. Owen, *A Sikh Family in Britain*, Religious Education Press 1973

Collick, E., *Through Grief*, Darton, Longman and Todd 1986

Department of Education and Science, *Curriculum 11–16*, 1977

Durkheim, E., *Suicide: A Study in Sociology*, ed. G. Simpson, Routledge 1952

Elias, N., *The Loneliness of the Dying*, trs. E. Jephcott, Blackwell 1985

Enright, D. J. (ed.), *The Oxford Book of Death*, OUP 1983

Fischer, E. and Marek, F., *Marx in His Own Words*, trs. A. Bostock, Penguin 1970

George, S., *How the Other Half Dies*, Penguin 1976

Gilbert, A., *Marx's Politics*, Martin Robertson 1981

Godin, A., *Death and Presence: The Psychology of Death and the Afterlife*, Lumen Vital Press 1966

Gorer, G., *Death, Grief and Mourning in Contemporary Britain*, The Cresset Press 1965

Grof, S. and C., *Beyond Death*, Thames and Hudson 1980

Grollman, E. A. (ed.), *Explaining Death to Children*, Beacon Press 1967

Harrison, S. W. and Shepherd, D., *A Muslim Family in Britain*, Religious Education Press 1979

Herod, F. G., *Who Cares?*, Methuen Educational 1981

Hick, J., *Death and Eternal Life*, Collins 1976

Holbrook, D., *The Secret Places*, Methuen 1965

Hughes, T. (ed.) *Sylvia Plath Collected Poems*, Faber 1981

Iqbal, M., *The Way of the Muslim*, Hulton Educational 1975

Iverson, J., *More Lives Than One?*, Souvenir Press 1976

Jacobs, L., *The Way of the Jews*, Hulton Educational 1981

Johnson, T. (ed.), *The Poems of Emily Dickinson*, Harvard University Press 1955

Kubler-Ross, E., *On Death and Dying*, Tavistock Publications 1973

Lampen, D., *Facing Death*, Quaker Home Service 1979

Ling, T. O., *Buddhism*, Ward Lock Educational 1980

Madge, V., *Children in Search of Meaning*, SCM Press 1965

Manning, D., *Don't Take My Grief Away*, Harper and Row 1985

McDermott, M. Y. and Ahsan, M. M., *The Muslim Guide*, Islamic Foundation 1980

McLeod, W. H., *The Way of the Sikh*, Hulton Educational 1975

Measham, D. C., *Fourteen: Autobiography of an Age-Group*, CUP 1965

Owen, R. J., *Christian Aid*, Religious and Moral Education Press 1983

Parkes, C. Murray and Weiss, R. S., *Recovery From Bereavement*, Basic Books 1983

Parrinder, E. G., *The Indestructible Soul*, Allen and Unwin 1973

Parrinder, E. G., *Something After Death*, Denholm House Press 1974

Piaget, J.,*The Child's Conception of the World*, trs. J. and A. Tomlinson, Routledge 1929

Pringle, D. D., *Christianity in Action Today*, Schofield and Sims 1971

Richardson, R. (ed.), *Losses: Talking About Bereavement*, Open Books 1980

Sarwar, G., *Islam: Beliefs and Teaching*, Muslim Educational Trust 1980

Schools Council, *Discovering an Approach*, 1977

Singh, Sir J., *Sikh Ceremonies*, Religious Book Society, Chandigarh, India 1968

Singh, T., *Sikhism, Its Ideals and Institutions*, Khalsa, Amritsar 1951

Smart, N., *Background to 'The Long Search'*, BBC 1977

Smart, N., *The Religious Experience of Mankind*, Fontana 1971

Taylor, E. J., *Problems of Christian Living*, Blackie 1978

Taylor, J. B., *Islam*, Lutterworth Educational 1971

Thomas, D., *The Poems*, Dent 1971

Toynbee, A. J. and Others, *Man's Concern With Death*, Hodder and Stoughton 1968

Twyford, A. and M., *Life and Death*, Association for Spina Bifida and Hydrocephalus 1983

Whaley, J. (ed.) *Mirrors of Mortality*, Europa Publications 1981

Winter, D. B., *Hereafter*, Hodder and Stoughton 1972

Wilson, I. and Bruce, R., *Life After Death*, Cassell Educational 1987

Yogashananda, Swami, *The Way of the Hindu*, Hulton Educational 1973

Articles

Alexander, I. E. and Alderstein, A. M. 'Affective Responses to the Concept of Death in a Population of Children and Adolescents', *The Journal of Genetic Psychology* 93, 1958, pp. 167–177.

Elkind, Dana, S. 'Varieties of Religious Experience in Young Adolescents', *The Journal for the Scientific Study of Religion* 11, 1962, pp. 102–112.

Godin, A. and Van Roey, B. 'Immanent Justice and Divine Protection', 1959.

Koocher, G. P. 'Childhood, Death and Cognitive Development', 1973.

Maurer, A. 'Maturation of Concepts of Death', *British Journal of Medical Psychology* 39, 35, 1966.

Maurer, A. 'The Child's Knowledge of Non-Existence', *Journal of Existentialist Psychiatry* 2, 1961, pp. 193–212.

Maurer, A. 'Adolescent Attitudes Toward Death', *The Journal of Genetic Psychology* 105, 1964, pp. 75–90.

Nagy, M. 'The Child's Theories Concerning Death', *The Journal of Genetic Psychology* 73, 1948, pp. 3–27.

Williams, R. L. and Cole, S. 'Religiosity, Generalized Anxiety, and Apprehension Concerning Death', *Journal of Social Psychology* 75, 1968, pp. 111–117.